MW00395471

UNDERSTANDING JOHN STUART MILL

The Smart Student's Guide to
Utilitarianism & On Liberty

Laurence D. Houlgate

Copyright © 2018 Laurence D. Houlgate

All rights reserved. No part of this book may be reproduced in any form or by any electronic or mechanical means, including information storage and retrieval systems, without written permission from the author, except in the case of a reviewer, who may quote brief passages embodied in critical articles or in a review.

Dedicated to the memory of
My dear friend and colleague
PATRICIA JOHNSON FORGIE

Other Books by Laurence Houlgate:
The Smart Student's Guides to Philosophical Classics:
Understanding Plato: The Smart Student's Guide to the Socratic Dialogues and the Republic
Understanding John Locke: The Smart Student's Guide to Second Treatise of Government

Philosophy of the Family:
The Child and the State: A Normative Theory of Juvenile Rights
Family and State: The Philosophy of Family Law
Morals, Marriage and Parenthood: An Introduction to Family Ethics
Philosophy, Law and the Family: A New Introduction to the Philosophy of Law

About the author:

Laurence Houlgate is Emeritus Professor of Philosophy at California Polytechnic State University in San Luis Obispo, California, where he taught philosophy for 38 years. He received M.A. and Ph.D. degrees in philosophy at the University of California, Los Angeles. Before his appointment at Cal Poly in 1979, he held professorships at the University of California (Santa Barbara), Reed College (Portland, Oregon) and George Mason University (Fairfax, Virginia). He lives in Paso Robles, California with his spouse, the poet Torre Houlgate-West, and indulges in his favorite hobbies: competing in U.S. Master and Senior Games swim meets and writing philosophy.

Acknowledgements:

I am grateful for the many helpful comments and suggestions of members of the SLO Night Writers (San Luis Obispo, California), most of whom are fiction writers who nonetheless sat patiently through several readings of parts of this book. And many thanks again to Judith Perrill Houlgate for her generous offer to proofread the penultimate draft of this book.

Cover design: Vila Designs (viladesigns.net)

A Modest Request:

Thank you for reading *Understanding John Stuart Mill*. If you like this book, please write a short review on my Amazon.com detail page: You can also visit my website at www.houlgatebooks.com and feel free to comment on my philosophical ramblings at https://houlgatebooks.blogspot.com/

Table of Contents

Preface

In 1980 members of the faculty of the Philosophy Department at California Polytechnic State University were asked to create an introductory course in philosophy that would be required of every student as part of their general education. The department voted to adopt my proposal to introduce students to philosophy by having them read only the original texts of pre-20th century classics of philosophy. At least one of the texts selected for the introductory course had to be from ancient philosophy and the remainder could be from any book of philosophy published before 1900, provided that it is generally regarded as a classic and accessible to beginning students. We created two 11-week courses based on this model. One course is devoted to classic works in ethics, social and political philosophy. The other course concentrates on classic works in epistemology and metaphysics. The authors typically chosen for these courses were the usual suspects: Plato, Aristotle, Descartes, Hobbes, Locke, Rousseau, Hume, Mill, Kant, and several other of the "great" philosophers.

Our hope in adopting this approach to introducing university students to philosophy was that they would not only learn about the nature of philosophy and philosophical method, but they would leave the course having read and (hopefully) understood some of the great books in Western philosophy; a rare accomplishment in a university with an enrollment of 20,000 students, most of them specializing in science or technology.

Looking back over the past 36 years I believe we achieved the latter objective but fell short in fulfilling the former. Most students would begin a course completely ignorant of the nature of philosophy, its questions and its methods. This is quite understandable, especially in light of the fact that most students have no exposure to philosophy before enrolling in the university. And yet, although our beginning students studied, discussed and were tested on their understanding of several classic works, it occurred to me that a high proportion of them would leave our courses unable to give coherent answers to such questions as: "What is philosophy?" "What is the nature of a philosophical problem?" "What methods does the philosopher use to resolve philosophical problems?" "How does a philosophical discovery differ from a discovery in science?" If students who completed a beginning course in biology or psychology were not able to define "biology," or "psychology," remained ignorant about the unique nature of a problem in these areas of study and could not explain some of the methods used to solve these problems, then their teacher would understandably declare the course to be a failure.

I soon decided that I would use a standard to judge the success or failure of my courses similar to the standard used by my hypothetical biology or psychology colleague. I would evaluate my own classes as a success if a majority of my students showed an understanding not only of the central ideas of each philosopher discussed, but they could also explain the nature of philosophy, how philosophical questions differed from those arising in the sciences, and (especially) the unique methods used by the great philosophers to solve these problems.

This book is the third of a series of student companions to the classics of Western philosophy that attempts to achieve these modest objectives. Each book in the series organizes the central claims of each classic text with the aim of clarifying the *kind* of question that the philosopher is asking and the *method(s)* the philosopher uses in the attempt to answer that question. I make no assumptions that the kind of question asked, or the method used to answer the question will always be the same as we move from one philosopher to another. What is important is that in the attempt to clarify the questions asked by each philosopher, students will be able to identify a common thread that will allow them to say "Ah yes, this is a question that is philosophical, not scientific. It does not call for the tools or methods typically used in scientific inquiry." If questions of philosophy are *not* to be resolved by observational research in the field or experimentation in the laboratory, then it will be important to determine how each philosopher goes about answering the questions posed. Once again, we might be able to find a common thread that allows a student to say "There, *that* is how philosophers go about their work." My hope is that a critical study of the classics will show that philosophy is *not* after all a random enterprise in which anyone can say whatever comes into their head because they believe there is no method on which to base a rational argument.

The series title is *Smart Student's Guides to Philosophical Classics*. The series is organized into volumes distinguished by the author under consideration. The first volume (*Understanding Plato*) presents issues and arguments in four of Plato's early ("Socratic") dialogues and in those parts of the *Republic* dealing with ethics and political philosophy. The second book is devoted to John Locke's moral and political theory in *Second Treatise of Government* (*Understanding John Locke*). As with previous volumes in this series, chapters in *Understanding John Stuart Mill* conclude with a set of questions for thought and discussion.

Although the student guides can be read on their own, my hope is that they will be read as *companions* to the original works of the philosophers discussed therein. I certainly do not recommend the guides as a substitute for a careful reading of the classic works. Students should always read the original text before looking at this or any other companion book for commentary and guidance about what the philosopher says or implies about the nature of philosophy, the important questions of philosophy and the methods of the philosopher for answering or attempting to answer these questions.

This volume introduces students to Mill's contribution to ethical theory (*Utilitarianism*) and political philosophy (*On Liberty*). Although *On Liberty* was published almost three years before the publication of *Utilitarianism*, we begin discussion in Part I with the latter volume. I do this because the liberty or harm-to-others principle is firmly grounded on both the principle of utility and individual rights, after the latter had been accommodated by Mill within the utility principle. Therefore, it is expedient to begin with *Utilitarianism* and give readers a firm understanding of the utilitarian theory of ethics before they dive into *On Liberty* in Part II.

A brief note about symbols, text boxes, comments, quotations and methods of attribution:

Shaded paragraphs (like this) are used instead of footnotes. They are mainly for clarifications, examples, comments or criticisms of Mill.

Chapters and chapter sections in this book are headed by Arabic numerals, for example: 8 and 8.1.1.

Chapters in Mill's *Utilitarianism* and On *Liberty* are indicated in parentheses, following the chapter number and name, for example: *Chapter 9 Society and the Individual (On Liberty IV)*.

Quotations from Mill are italicized and indented. The page numbers cited are from the Hackett paper editions of *Utilitarianism* (ed. G. Sher) and *On Liberty* (ed. E. Rapaport).

Quotations from authors (other than Locke) are placed in parentheses indicating the name of the author and page number quoted -- for example: **(Houlgate, 18)**. The complete reference with author name, date of publication, book title, name of publisher and place of publication can be found in *References*, at the end of each chapter. Bibliographies for further reading can be found at the end of Parts I and II.

Please consult the *Glossary* at the end of the document for definitions of technical terms. If a word in the text is to be found in the glossary then that word will be in **bold face** type.

About John Stuart Mill

"I have no remembrance of the time when I began to learn Greek; I have been told that it was when I was three years old."   (J.S. Mill, *Autobiography*)

And so began John Stuart Mill's education, tutored entirely at home by his father, who took advantage of his son's extraordinary intelligence to train him to become next in line to carry the flag for radical legal and social change in England.

John was born on 20 May 1806 in northeast London, the eldest of six children. His father was James Mill, a Scotsman, who had been educated at Edinburgh University. James had moved to London in 1802, "where he was to become a friend and prominent ally of Jeremy Bentham and the Philosophical Radicals" who were urging extreme changes in the social order. It has been said that the education of John was motivated by the desire of his father, encouraged and supported by Bentham, now John's godfather, to equip young John not only for leadership of the next generation of radicalism, but to guarantee that Bentham's ground-breaking work in philosophy, economics and political theory would survive long after his death. To this end, James' education of his son was a huge success. The writings of John Stuart Mill, including *Utilitarianism* and *On Liberty*, have had a strong influence on ethics and political philosophy and are now considered essential reading not only for philosophy and political science students, but for anyone who wants to study philosophical classics and to accept the challenge to think critically about moral principles and individual liberty.

James Mill recognized soon after John's birth that he and his wife (Elizabeth Barrow) had produced a genius. Despite his own work doing his rigorous research while writing the seven-volume *A History of British India*, James immediately set himself to home-schooling young John.

After John learned Greek and studied mathematics, between the ages of four and nine John read, on a daily basis, books of history, beginning with the histories of ancient Greece, Rome, Scotland and England. John would take long walks with his father in the early morning before breakfast. He would give his father an account of the books he had read the day before, referring to notes he had made on slips of paper while reading.

John had absorbed most of the classical canon by age twelve—along with algebra, Euclid, and the major Scottish and English historians. In his early teenage years, he studied political economy, logic, and calculus, utilizing his spare time to digest treatises on experimental science as an amusement. At age fifteen—upon returning from a year-long trip to France, a nation he would eventually call home—he started work on the major treatises of philosophy, psychology and government (Macleod, citing Reeves 11–27).

At age seventeen, instead of going to university (Oxford or Cambridge), where he would have certainly been a great success, John's occupation and status was set for the next thirty-five years by his father's obtaining for him "an appointment from the East India Company, in the office of the Examiner of India Correspondence" (*Autobiography*). His first job was to serve as a junior clerk to his father, who years earlier had received the same position on the basis of his authorship of *A History of British India*. John dove into his work while at the same time continuing his studies at home, tutoring his brothers and sisters, taking on the responsibility of editing Bentham's newest book, and publicly propagandizing for the radical politics agenda.

All of this took its toll. At age twenty John lapsed into a deep depression. His education had prepared him for writing about and promoting the creed of the Philosophical Radicals, but it had not prepared him for life.

> [I]t occurred to me to put the question directly to myself: "Suppose that all your objects in life were realized; that all the changes in institutions and opinions which you are looking forward to, could be completely effected at this very instant: would this be a great joy and happiness to you?" And an irrepressible self-consciousness distinctly answered, "No!"
>
> I seemed to have nothing left to live for. These were the thoughts which mingled with the dry, heavy dejection of the melancholy winter of 1826-7. During this time, I was not incapable of my usual occupations. I went on with them mechanically, by the mere force of habit. I had been so drilled in a certain sort of mental exercise, that I could still carry it on when all the spirit had gone out of it...
>
> [A friend] told me how he and others had looked upon me as a "made" or manufactured man, having had a certain impress of opinion stamped on me which I could only reproduce. (*Autobiography*)

Mill's depression continued for three years. These episodes were to recur throughout his life. His first recovery from (what he called) "the malaise" began with an "accidental" reading of Marontel's *Memoires*.

> [I] came to the passage which relates his [Marontel's] father's death, the distressed position of the family, and the sudden inspiration by which he, then a mere boy, felt and made them feel that he would be everything to them--would supply the place of all that they had lost. A vivid conception of the scene and its feelings came over me, and I was moved to tears. From this moment my burden became lighter. The oppression of the thought that all feeling was dead within me was gone. I was no longer hopeless: I was not

a stock of stone. I had still, it would seem, some of the material out of which all worth of character, and all capacity for happiness, are made. (Autobiography)

The poetry and writings of Coleridge, Carlyle, and Goethe opened the door to Romantic thought and an acute awareness that the Enlightenment philosophy with which he had been brought up only contained "one side of the truth" (*Autobiography*). He later recounted in *On Liberty*, his most famous book, that no one should ever claim certainty for any philosophical theory, school or position, including the utilitarian creed he had been promoting for several years. Mill set as a personal goal to reconcile Romanticism and Utilitarianism. "[W]hoever could master the premises and combine the methods of both, would possess the entire English philosophy of their age" (Mill, "Coleridge").

A few years after his emotional restoration, Mill met Harriet Taylor at a dinner party in 1830, and the two quickly fell in love. Unfortunately for both, Harriet had, four years' prior, married John Taylor—"an amiable, though intellectually unadventurous, pharmacist." In fact, Taylor was so amiable that he responded to the couple's mutual desire to be with each other with a generous offer to disappear on occasion and leave the two alone. For several years, Mill visited Harriet at the Taylors' country retreat when Harriet's husband was not present, and at their London residence while he visited his Club. Although Mill and Harriet insisted that their relationship was entirely platonic, not everyone agreed.

Our relation to each other at that time was one of strong affection and confidential intimacy only. For though we did not consider the ordinances of society binding on a subject so entirely personal, we did feel bound that our conduct should be such as in no degree to bring discredit on her husband, nor therefore on herself. (Autobiography)

During these years of platonic courtship, Mill wrote *A System of Logic* (1843), *Principles of Political Economy* (1848), and published weekly opinion pieces for the London newspapers. He was also an editor of and frequent contributor to the *London and Westminster Review*, a quarterly journal founded and funded by Jeremy Bentham in 1823 (Ousby).

Harriet's husband died in 1849. Two years later Harriet and Mill married, "though not before the perceived scandal had caused a rift between Mill and many of his friends. Mill felt first-hand the stifling effect of Victorian judgmentalism and oppressive norms of propriety—a subject he would later take up in *On Liberty*" (Macleod).

Harriet was an enthusiastic participant in Mill's writings during the next several years. Mill credits her with making major corrections and revisions of the first drafts of what would become Mill's central ideas.

[On Liberty] was more directly and literally our joint production than anything else which bears my name, for there was not a sentence of it that was not several times gone through by us together, turned over in many ways, and carefully weeded of any faults, either in thought or expression, that we detected in it. It is in consequence of this that, although it never underwent her final revision, it far surpasses, as a mere specimen of composition, anything which has proceeded from me either before or since. With regard to the thoughts, it is difficult to identify any particular part or element as being more hers than all the rest. The whole mode of thinking of which the book was the expression, was emphatically hers (Autobiography).

Harriet died in 1858, only seven and one-half years after their marriage, while Mill and she were travelling through France. Harriet was buried in Avignon. Mill was devastated. He purchased a house in Avignon, close to the cemetery, where he would live out most of the rest of his life. He inscribed on her grave that

[s]he was the sole earthly delight of those who had the happiness to belong to her. [...] Were there but a few hearts and intellects like hers this earth would already become the hoped-for heaven.

Harriet's death, in fact, came only a little over a month after Mill's retirement from the East India Company, for which he had worked for almost thirty-five years. At the time of his retirement, Mill had risen through the ranks, eventually holding his father's former position of Chief Examiner of Correspondence—"a position roughly equivalent to Undersecretary of State, involving managing dispatches for colonial administration" (Macleod, quoting Zastoupil 1994).

After Harriet's death, and probably at her urging before she died, Mill continued writing. After publishing *On Liberty*, the year after her death, *Utilitarianism* appeared in *Fraser's Magazine* in three installments in 1861. In the same year he published *Considerations on Representative Government*. Four years later Mill wrote *An Examination of Sir William Hamilton's Philosophy* (1865), and at the urging and help of his step-daughter Helen Taylor, Mill wrote *On the Subjection of Women* (1869), one of the first and most influential books promoting the legal and social equality of women. Mill's *Autobiography* was published in the year of his death (1873).

In 1865, Mill was urged by the Liberal Party to stand for membership in the British Parliament, as a representative of Westminster district. Here is how he responded, campaigned and won the seat:

I wrote, in reply to the offer, a letter for publication, saying that I had no personal wish to be a member of Parliament, that I thought a candidate ought neither to canvass nor to incur any expense, and that I could not consent to do either. I said further, that if elected, I could not undertake to give any of my time and labour to their local interests. With respect to general politics..., I made known to them, among other things, my conviction ... that women were entitled to representation in Parliament on the same terms with men. It was the first time, doubtless, that such a doctrine had ever been mentioned to English electors; and the fact that I was elected after proposing it, gave the start to the movement which has since become so vigorous, in favour of women's suffrage...

I strictly adhered to [my plan], neither spending money nor canvassing, nor did I take any personal part in the election, until about a week preceding the day of nomination, when I attended a few public meetings to state my principles and give to any questions which the electors might exercise their just right of putting to me for their own guidance; answers as plain and unreserved as my address [Mill had spent most of his time during the period preceding his return to England at his home in Avignon]. (*Autobiography*).

While in the House of Commons, Mill did exactly what he had promised. He championed the unpopular causes of extension of suffrage to women, Irish reform, and the prosecution of Governor Eyre for atrocities committed during his administration of Jamaica. As a result of his strong support for the prosecution of the governor, he frequently received abusive letters: "They graduated from coarse jokes, verbal and pictorial, up to threats of assassination" (*Autobiography*).

Mill did not win a second term, being defeated in 1868 (Kinzer, Robson, and Robson 1992). He retired to his home in Avignon. He died there on 7 May 1873, at age 67, and was buried next to his beloved wife Harriet.

References

Macleod, Christopher, "John Stuart Mill", The Stanford Encyclopedia of Philosophy (Spring 2018 Edition), Edward N. Zalta (ed.)

Mill, J.S. 1873. *Autobiography*. London: Longmans, Green, Reader, and Dyer.

Mill, J.S. 1840. Coleridge, in *The Collected Works of John Stuart Mill, Volume X—Essays on Ethics, Religion, and Society*, ed. John M. Robson. Toronto: University of Toronto Press; London: Routledge and Kegan Paul, 1985.

Ousby, I. 1995. Ed., *The Cambridge Guide to Literature in English*. Cambridge University Press,1008.

Reeves, R., 2007, *John Stuart Mill: Victorian Firebrand*, London: Atlantic Books.

Zastoupil, L., 1994, *John Stuart Mill and India*. Stanford, CA: Stanford University Press.

"Whatever the subject, Mill surveys the ground, clears it of underbrush, builds a house of straw to demonstrate what a shoddy house looks like, sets it on fire, and in its place builds a house of brick, which he dares you to knock down. The house of brick is, as Victorian brick houses usually were, lacking in grace and lightness and charm, but it still stands. You don't come away from Mill dazzled, as you do with Ruskin or Carlyle, but you come away with a place to live your life."   Adam Gopnik

JOHN STUART MILL

PART I *UTILITARIANISM*

Chapter 1 General Remarks (*Utilitarianism* I)

Mill begins by reflecting on "the little progress" that has been made by philosophers about the "criterion of right and wrong." He writes that the debate has been going on for more than two thousand years and the same schools of thought are still locked in a "vigorous warfare" about the foundations of morality.

1.1 First principles in science and philosophy

Mill points out that the controversy about first principles is not unique to philosophy. There is a similar debate that goes on in the sciences, including mathematics. However, unlike the debate in philosophy, the outcome of the debates in the sciences does not impair "the trustworthiness of the conclusions of those sciences" (*Utilitarianism*, 1). This is because "the doctrines of a science are not usually deduced from, nor depend on their evidence upon, what are called its first principles" (2).

> "The relation of the first principles of a science is not that of foundations to an edifice, but of roots to a tree, which may perform their office equally well though they be never dug down to and exposed to light" (2).

In other words, we can get along perfectly well in science without ever contemplating or even knowing anything about the laws of identity, non-contradiction, and excluded middle.

Examples of first principles of science (also known as Laws of Thought):
The law of identity: "Whatever is, is."
The law of non-contradiction: "Nothing can both be and not be."
The law of excluded middle: "Everything must either be or not be."

But this is not the case when making a moral judgement:

> All action is for the sake of some end, and rules of action, it seems natural to suppose, must take their whole character and color from the end to which they are subservient... A test of right and wrong must be the means, one would think, of ascertaining what is right or wrong, and not a consequence of having already ascertained it (2).

Thus, to whether an action is right or wrong ("Would it be wrong to break my promise to visit my friend in the hospital?"), I need a "test" or "rule" of right and wrong to answer the question (for example, the rule "One ought not to break a promise"). We use moral rules to judge whether what we do is right or wrong. I do not say that breaking the promise to my friend is wrong, and then *create* or attempt to create a rule to justify what I did. Instead, I use an existing rule *as a means* of ascertaining that what I did is right or wrong.

But Mill is saying more than this. The *first principles* of morals and legislation have the same foundational role as moral rules. These first principles, as proposed by all theories, are the foundations (the means) from which *moral rules* are derived.

Mill claims that the first principles of morals and legislation are "foundations to an edifice." Unlike the first principles of science, they *do not* perform their office unless they are "exposed to light." Only when we expose them will we be able to make *rational* moral judgements.

> Examples of first principles of morals:
> "One ought to act only in accordance with a maxim that one can at the same time will as a universal law" (Kant)
> "No one ought to harm another in his life, health, liberty or possessions" (Locke)
> "Actions are right in proportion as they tend to promote happiness; wrong as they tend to produce the reverse of happiness" (Mill)

1.2 Intuitive and inductive ways of knowing moral truth

> The "schools of thought" to which Mill referred in 1.1 are the intuitive and the inductive. Both schools agree on "the necessity of general laws," but disagree on "their evidence and the source from which they derive their authority" (3).
> Most philosophers today prefer to use **deontology** and **consequentialism** for the names of the contending ethical theories, reserving "intuitive" and "inductive" for the way in which one claims to know that the law in question is true or false.

(a) There are two branches of the intuitive school. The first branch claims that everyone has a natural faculty, a "sense of instinct" that allows them to perceive that particular actions are right or wrong, in the same way that we hear the sound of a bell or see the first light of morning.

Without telling us why this "popular theory" would be rejected by anyone with "a pretension to philosophy," Mill quickly moves on to a discussion of a second branch of intuitionist theory. This version says that we have a natural faculty that allows us to discern, not what is right or wrong in particular cases, but only what *general principles* of moral judgment are true or false. Moral intuition "is a branch of our reason, not of our sensitive faculty." The faculty of reason allows us to say (for example) "There is a law of nature that tells us we ought not to harm others in their life, health, liberty or possessions" (John Locke). I do not instinctively know that an act of forcible rape is morally wrong, but I do intuitively know that the moral rule or principle that obliges us not to perform such acts is true.

The intuitive school has much in common with the inductive school, its' main opponent. Both schools agree that it is necessary to have general moral laws, and both agree "that the morality of an individual action is not a question of direct perception, but of the application of a law to an individual case" (2). Both schools also endorse almost the same set of moral rules, for example, the obligation to tell the truth, to keep promises, to refrain from killing or physically harming others, to not steal or damage the possessions of others, to not restrict their liberty.

The major difference between the intuitive and inductive schools is about *how one knows* that general moral laws or principles are true or false. Intuitionists argue that true principles of morals are known *a priori*, in the same way that a definition is known to be true. For example, to know that a triangle is a 3-sided plane figure all we need to know is the meaning of the terms in the definition. There is no need to observe or experience triangles. By analogy (claims the intuitionist) one can know *a priori* that *murder is wrong* because the word "murder" means "wrongful killing." One can also know *a priori* that *breaking a promise is wrong* because (for example) "I promise to meet with you tomorrow" is to place myself under a moral obligation to meet with you, "breaking a promise" is to violate the obligation and this is equivalent to wrongdoing.

However, it gets much more complicated for the intuitive school if we move from the level of individual actions to the level of first principles. Thus, to know that there is a universal moral obligation not to kill either oneself or other human beings (except in self-defense), it is not clear that we can do this by a simple analysis of the words "human being," "killing oneself," "killing others," and "moral obligation."

(b) According to the inductive school, "right and wrong, as well as truth and falsehood, are questions of observation and experience" (3). Mill does not give an example, but we can construct one by assuming that the words "right" and "wrong" signify the result of an *inductive argument* based on observing and measuring the good and bad consequences of human behavior. As Mill will inform us in the next chapter, this can be done if we assume that the word "good" means "pleasure," and the word "bad" means "pain." Thus, if asked whether it would be morally right to tell a lie to save a person's life, someone who favors the inductive approach would answer by first calculating the amounts of pleasure and pain that would be caused by telling the lie and compare this to the amounts of pleasure and pain caused by not telling the lie. They would then look to see what course of action would cause a "greater balance" of pleasure over pain. Observation and experience is all one would need to make the relevant calculations, and thereby to answer the question about right and wrong.

Mill concludes this lengthy paragraph by reminding us that although the intuitive agrees with the inductive school that there is a science of morals, "they seldom attempt to make out a list of the *a priori* principles which are to serve as the premises of the science," either by citing one first principle, or if there are several, telling us which has precedence over the others "when they conflict" (3).

1.3 The indispensability of utility-based arguments

Mill observes that "men's sentiments, both of favor and of aversion, are greatly influenced by what they supposed to be the effects of things upon their happiness" (3). This observation should not surprise us. One person is in favor of early morning walks because it makes him happy, while another person is averse to this activity because she would rather sleep in the early morning. This explains why the principle of utility (also known as "the greatest happiness principle") has had such a strong effect even on the moral doctrines "of those who most scornfully reject its authority" (3).

To give one example of the indispensability of utilitarian arguments, Mill turns to the German philosopher Immanuel Kant's first principle of morals, called the *categorical imperative*. It has several versions, the first being "one ought to act only in accordance with a maxim that one can at the same time will to become a universal law."

Kant does not claim that the categorical imperative can be known to be true merely by analyzing the meaning of its terms. Instead, he argues that if we want to discover whether an act ought to be done, we must ask whether a person could will, *without contradiction*, that everyone act as he or she is acting.

Kant uses the example of a lying promise. Suppose you are a poor college student who is living in a dorm room with another student who is very rich. You do not have enough money to pay tuition for the next semester. You ask your rich roommate for a loan. He agrees to loan you the money but only if you promise to repay him by the end of the semester. You know that you cannot keep this promise, but you go ahead and make the promise anyway. This is what Kant calls a "lying promise."

It is wrong to make a lying promise because (Kant writes) it is *logically impossible* to will that everyone could make a lying promise whenever they need to borrow money or to escape any other difficulty. When the lying promise was made, your aim in making was it to convince your roommate that you would repay the loan. You wanted him or her to "credit" your promise. But if everyone else made lying promises under the same circumstances, then no one would believe that promises would be kept. The liar could not consistently will that his maxim be a universal law because this would frustrate his aim in aim making the lying promise. Therefore, Kant concludes that *one ought not* to escape a difficulty (needing tuition money) by making a lying promise.

Mill takes issue with Kant's reasoning about the *a priori* status of the categorical imperative. Mill does not think that "there would be any contradiction, any logical impossibility, in the adoption by all rational beings of the most outrageously immoral rules of conduct." Instead, Mill goes on to say, "All he shows is that the *consequences of their universal adoption would be such as no one would choose to incur,*" proving Mill's initial point that appeals to utility are indispensable.

1.4 Two meanings of the word "proof"

Mill announces that his aim in *Utilitarianism* is to help his readers understand and appreciate the utilitarian theory--and to contribute something "toward such proof as it is susceptible of" (4).

He cautions his readers that the proof of the theory will not be ***direct.*** "Questions of ultimate ends are not amenable to direct proof" (4). If it is said that something is good, then it is assumed that this is so because it is a means to something else that is good, or it is good in itself. If you go to the opera because you find it enjoyable, and I ask you why you seek enjoyment, you would understandably wonder whether I am joking. Enjoyment (pleasure) is an ultimate end, and as such cannot be proved. If you must go to the dentist to have an infected tooth pulled, it makes sense to say that this is good, but only because it is a means to the relief of your tooth pain. If we further ask, "Why do you want your pain relieved," you would have no answer. The relief of pain is an ultimate end. As an ultimate end, there is by definition, no way to directly prove that this end is good.

> *If, then, it is asserted that there is a comprehensive formula, including all things which are in themselves good, and that whatever else is good is not so as an end but as a means, the formula may be accepted or rejected, but is not a subject of what is commonly understood by proof* (4).

But fear not, fellow philosophers, for Mill rescues us from the despair of making an arbitrary choice of one comprehensive formula over another. He does this by proposing "a larger meaning of the word 'proof'" (4), a meaning of this word that that we can all understand: "Considerations may be presented capable of determining the intellect either to give or withhold assent to the doctrine: and this is equivalent to proof" (5).

What are these **considerations**? Whose intellect do we consult? What if my intellect gives consent to the doctrine and yours does not? Mill does not answer these questions until Chapter IV.

1.5 Questions for thought and discussion

1. Mill says that the first version of the claim that we know right or wrong by intuition is not even worthy of philosophical discussion. Is he right about this? Is it worthwhile to discuss a theory that says we perceive right and wrong in the same way we perceive the sound of a bell?

2. Is Mill correct in his criticism of Kant? Is the categorical imperative just a disguised attempt to show the bad consequences of making a lying promise? Or is Kant correct in thinking that it is logically impossible (contradictory) to will that everyone ought to go about making lying promises?

3. Are you convinced by Mill that the first principles of science have no impact on what scientists do in their laboratories, even though the first principles of morals are a necessary means to making rational moral judgments?

4. Explain Mill's distinction between direct and indirect proofs for a theory of ultimate ends.

Chapter 2 What Utilitarianism Is (*Utilitarianism* II)

The title speaks for itself. After scolding "the common herd of writers" for constantly misusing the word "utility" Mill offers the following definition:

> *The creed which accepts as the foundation of morals "utility" or the "greatest happiness principle" holds that actions are right in proportion as they tend to promote happiness, wrong as they tend to produce the reverse of happiness. By happiness is intended pleasure and the absence of pain; by unhappiness, pain and the privation of pleasure (7).*

Our actions tend to produce happiness (pleasure) and unhappiness (pain). If an action produces at least as much happiness as unhappiness than any other action that could have been performed in the same circumstances, then the action is *morally right*. If the action produces more unhappiness than happiness than any other action that could have been performed, then the action is *morally wrong*. It is a *moral obligation* to refrain from performing actions that are morally wrong.

2.1 The utilitarian theory of life

Embedded in the definition is the assumption that the only consequence of an act or omission that counts is *happiness*, defined above as "pleasure and freedom from pain," and *unhappiness*, defined as "pain and the privation of pleasure."

> *...pleasure and freedom from pain are the only things desirable as ends; and...all desirable things (which are as numerous in the utilitarian as any other scheme) are desirable either for pleasure inherent in themselves or as means to the promotion of pleasure and the prevention of pain (7).*

This statement about what things are *desirable as ends* is what Mill refers to as the utilitarian "theory of life."

> The utilitarian theory of life is also known as **hedonism** -- the philosophical theory that pleasure is the highest good and proper aim of human life. The Epicurean school founded in Athens by Epicurus, advocated hedonism (pleasure as the highest good), but of a restrained kind: mental pleasure was regarded more highly than physical, and the ultimate pleasure was held to be freedom from anxiety and mental pain, especially that arising from needless fear of death and of the gods." (Oxford)

Here is an example of how the utilitarian principle might be used to evaluate an action as right or wrong. Suppose that Maria breaks a promise to help her friend Juan study for the philosophy final exam. She realizes at the last moment that she needs that time to help her ailing mother at home. Juan is disappointed, but not overly stressed about the broken promise because he is fairly certain he can find another tutor. She is happy that she now has more time to help at home, even though he is mildly unhappy ("disappointed") not to study with a friend. Given these facts, Maria's action (breaking the promise) probably produces more total happiness for Maria and her mother than it produces unhappiness for Juan. To put it another way, the action of breaking the promise produces a greater balance of pleasure over pain than would be produced by the alternative action of keeping her promise. Breaking the promise is **optimific.** Hence, Maria's act of breaking the promise to Juan is not morally wrong.

In the 1930s, scholars began to use the adjective "optimific", meaning "producing the maximum good consequences." (Oxford English Dictionary)

Mill has much more to say about the definition of utility as he clarifies it through rebuttals to a large variety of misunderstandings and misrepresentations of the utilitarian "creed." We begin with a long section on objections and replies (2.2) and conclude this chapter with a summary of what we have learned about utilitarianism from Mill's rebuttals (2.3).

2.2 Objections and replies

Mill describes and replies to eight objections to the utilitarian theory.

2.2.1 The utilitarian theory of life sets a standard that is too low for human beings

The first objection is directed at the utilitarian theory of life:

To suppose that life has (as they express it) no higher end than pleasure—no better and nobler object of desire and pursuit—they designate as utterly mean and groveling, as a doctrine worthy only of swine... (7)

Mill immediately responds that this accusation makes the dubious assumption that "humans are capable of no pleasures except those of which swine are capable" (7). If this supposition were true, then the accusation could not be denied, but it would lose its force as an accusation: "If the sources of pleasure were precisely the same to human beings and to swine, the rule of life which is good enough for the one would be good enough for the other" (8).

The assumption is false. The reason why we think that the pleasures of the swine are "utterly mean and groveling" is that "a beast's pleasures do not satisfy a human being's conception of happiness."

Human beings have faculties more elevated than the animal appetites and, when once made conscious of them, do not regard anything as happiness which does not include their gratification. (8)

Mill distinguishes between *mental* and *bodily* pleasures. Examples of mental pleasures are "pleasures of the intellect, of the feelings and imagination, and the moral sentiments" (8). The bodily pleasures are the pleasures of "mere sensation," that is, the pleasures humans feel when satisfying "the animal appetites" (thirst, hunger, sexual urges).

At this point in the discussion Mill has successfully rebutted the swine objection to the utilitarian theory of life. If swine are not capable of the pleasures of which humans are capable, then the theory that pleasure and freedom of pain are the only things desirable as ends is immunized against accusations that the utilitarian theory of life is "mean and groveling."

But Mill wants to go further than this. He wants to prove not only that the mental pleasures experienced by humans are not experienced by beasts, but that the mental pleasures are *superior* to the bodily pleasures that both humans and beasts alike experience. Thus, the pleasures of gratifying a bodily appetite will always rank lower on the standard of superiority than the mental pleasures of the intellect.

2.2.1.1 Standards of superiority and inferiority

There are two standards of superiority and inferiority when ranking pleasures of the body and of the mind. The first standard is *quantitative*. It ranks mental and bodily pleasures by their intensity and duration, and also by such "circumstantial advantages" as their permanence, safety, costliness and other measurable factors. Although Mill writes that "on all these points utilitarians have fully proved their case," he does not provide any empirical data. Perhaps what he has in mind is the greater monetary cost of satisfying our appetites for food and drink than the cost of satisfying our desire for intellectual stimulation. We need to pay for food and drink, but we do not have to pay anyone for the pleasure of thinking about the problems of philosophy.

Mill's mentor Jeremy Bentham declared that the value of a pleasure is a measurable function of its intensity and duration. Using these factors alone, Bentham denied that the "higher" pleasures are the more valuable: "Prejudice apart, the game of push-pin is of equal value with the arts and sciences of music and poetry. If the game of push-pin furnishes more pleasure, it is more valuable than either. Everybody can play at push-pin: poetry and music are relished only by a few." (Bentham, 94).

The *qualitative* standard for ranking different kinds of pleasure is based on the preference of those persons who have experienced both mental and physical pleasures. The preference for one over the other must not be based on an obligation to prefer it, and it must be the preference of persons who are *competently* acquainted with both kinds of pleasure (that is, unlike a child or someone who is mentally handicapped, they must understand their experience--mere exposure to the pleasure is not sufficient). If they know that "a great amount" of discontent would be involved and yet they would still prefer it, then "we are justified in ascribing to the preferred enjoyment a superiority in quality, so far outweighing quantity as to render it, in comparison, of small account" (8-9)

Mill's approach to establishing a qualitative standard for ranking types of pleasure is reminiscent of Plato's method of ranking the three pleasures of learning, victory or honor, and making a profit. He has Socrates arguing that the only way to judge which of these is "the best" is to consult those who have experienced each pleasure and are experts in "knowledge and argument." It is not surprising that Socrates declares that the only persons who qualify as judges are those who love learning (the philosophers), not those who love honor or making a profit (Republic, 582a).

2.2.1.2 Application of the qualitative standard

We can reasonably expect that when Mill applies his standard of superiority to the bodily and mental pleasures, he will find that the mental pleasures rank higher. But notice that in the quote that follows, Mill does not exactly do this:

Now it is an unquestionable fact that those who are equally acquainted with and equally capable of appreciating and enjoying both do give a most marked preference to the manner of existence which employed their higher faculties. Few human creatures would consent to be changed into any of the lower animals for a promise of the fullest allowance of a beast's pleasures; no intelligent person would consent to be a fool; no instructed person would be an ignoramus (9).

Notice the subtle switch from comparing two different types of pleasure (mental and bodily) to comparing two "manners of existence." Instead of giving empirical evidence that persons competently acquainted with mental and bodily pleasures would almost always prefer the mental pleasure, Mill attempts to show something else. He tries to persuade us that once acquainted with *the life* of the intelligent person and *the life* of the fool, most of us would choose the former. But that is not what Mill promised to prove. He had promised to give empirical evidence for the former claim about specific mental and bodily pleasures.

There is probably good reason for this feint from the comparison of kinds of pleasures to the comparison of kinds of lives. Mill must have been aware that there are many counter-examples of persons "competently acquainted" with a large variety of mental and bodily pleasures but would choose the latter. For example, let us suppose that the newlyweds Percival and Griselda are "competently acquainted" with the bodily pleasures of sexual intercourse and the mental pleasures of thinking about philosophical problems (they have both recently graduated with Bachelor of Arts degrees in philosophy). When asked, they place their mutual pleasures of sexual intercourse so far above the pleasure of thinking about philosophical problems that they prefer the former. Moreover, at this early stage of their marriage, they "would not resign it for any quantity of the mental pleasure which their nature is capable of."

It might be objected to the preceding example that this is only one instance of persons choosing a bodily pleasure over a mental pleasure. There are many more examples we could give. The choice of examples depends upon what "competent acquaintance and experience" means and the social circumstances of the persons who are evaluating their experiences. If it is the degree of competence and acquaintance of John Stuart Mill and his highly educated friends in mid-nineteenth century England, then it is doubtful that they would give a "decided preference" to a bodily pleasure as the "more desirable pleasure." But suppose we choose a group of American college students who have experienced both kinds of pleasure and are acquainted with both. If asked whether they would prefer to "party" on Saturday night or stay at home and discuss Hegel, I would wager a sizeable bet that most of them would prefer the former. If asked, they would insist that going to a party on a Saturday night is a "more desirable pleasure."

I think we can all agree that Mill is on firmer ground when he discusses and compares the *manner of existence* of a human being to that of a fool and a pig:

> *It is better to be a human being dissatisfied than a pig satisfied; better to be Socrates dissatisfied than a fool satisfied. And if the fool, or the pig, are of a different opinion, it is because they only know their own side of the question. The other party to the comparison knows both sides* (10).

I do not know how to get this information from a fool or a pig, but hypothetically I would conjecture that if a human being is feeling quite miserable after the loss of a loved one and he is offered the opportunity to have a lobotomy, thereby reducing his mental capacity to that of a fool or pig, he not would take the offer, even if assured that his bodily needs would be satisfied for the rest of his pig-like life.

2.2.2 *The utilitarian theory of life is irrational*

Mill writes that a common objection to the utilitarian theory of life is that "happiness cannot be the rational purpose of human life" because (a) happiness is not attainable, and (b) even if it is attainable, humans should renounce happiness as a necessary condition of achieving virtue.

2.2.2.1 Verbal quibbles

Mill's reply to (a) is that the objection rests on a confusion of two meanings of the word "happiness." If by this word the objector means "a continuity of highly pleasurable excitement," then "it is evident enough that this is impossible." Someone might be able to make a state of "exalted pleasure" last for moments, or even hours or days, but it is psychologically impossible to make this kind of pleasure a permanent, long-lasting experience.

There is another meaning of "happiness." It is what an elderly person might mean when she reflects on her past and says, "I have had a happy life." She would probably not mean "a life of rapture,"

> ... but moments of such, in an existence made up of few and transitory pains, many and various pleasures, with a decided predominance of the active over the passive and having as the foundation of the whole not to expect more from life than it is capable of bestowing (13).

Mill says that there are many persons who have achieved this kind of life, and it is "worthy of the name of happiness." He conjectures that "the present wretched education and wretched social arrangements" in the mid-nineteenth century explains why happiness is not attainable by "almost all" (13).

2.2.2.2 The obligation to renounce one's own happiness

It is certainly *possible* to do without happiness in one's life. Mill writes (somewhat sarcastically) that this is done involuntarily "by nineteen-twentieths of mankind, even in those parts of our present world which are least deep in barbarism" (15). But it is also done voluntarily "by the hero or the martyr, for the sake of something which he prizes more than his individual happiness."

The relevant question is whether there is an *obligation* to renounce one's own happiness. The hero or the martyr does not sacrifice himself just for the sake of self-sacrifice. He does it "for the sake of something which he prizes more than his individual happiness," for example, the happiness of a loved one or for the good of his country (15). The sacrifice is a means to an end, not its own end.

This is not to deny that there are some people who renounce their own happiness just for the sake of renouncing it. The ascetic mounted on his pillar "may be an inspiring proof of what men *can* do, but assuredly it is not an example of what they *should* do (16).

If it is argued that the self-sacrifice is a means to attaining not happiness but virtue, which is better than happiness, Mill asks,

> *Would the sacrifice be made if the hero or martyr did not believe that it would earn for others immunity from similar sacrifices? Would it be made if he thought that his renunciation of happiness for himself would produce no fruit for any of his fellow creatures...?* (16).

The ascetic's sacrifice is *wasted* if it "does not increase the sum total of happiness" (16). The only self-renunciation which the utilitarian applauds is "devotion to the happiness or to some of the means of happiness, of others, either of mankind collectively or of individuals within the limits imposed by the collective interests of mankind" (16).

Mill concludes his reply to the objection by reminding the reader that "the utilitarian standard of what is right in conduct is not the agent's own happiness, but that of all concerned" (16). When making a calculation about the amount of pleasure and pain that might be caused by doing action P rather than actions Q and R, the agent must *impartially* consider the pleasure and pain of *all persons affected*, not just his own pleasure and pain. In this way, the utilitarian morality accepts and matches the ideal perfection of the golden rule: "To do as you would be done by," and "to love your neighbor as yourself."

2.2.3 The utilitarian standard sets a standard that is too high for human beings

It is sometimes argued that the utilitarian standard is "too high" for most persons to ever attain. The moral requirement that we always act "from the inducement" of promoting the greatest good of all persons who might be affected by our conduct exacts too much from ordinary people.

Mill responds that we should notice, first that this is the exact opposite of the objection at 2.1.1 where it was said that the utilitarian theory of life was "too low" a standard for human beings.

Second, this objection confuses the *rule of action* with the *motive* of it. The utilitarian is *not* asking us to make judgements about right or wrong by considering the motive (inducement) that propelled a person to do what she did. Instead, the theory demands only that one should do the act that promotes the greatest happiness.

The application of the utilitarian rule has nothing to do with motive. Mill uses the example of saving someone from drowning. Suppose that the rescuer's motive is the hope of getting a substantial reward for his efforts. If asked whether the rescuer did the morally right thing by saving the rescued person's life, we would not hesitate to say that he did, even if we knew that the rescuer's motive was not a feeling of duty, but self-interest. "It is the business of ethics to tell us what are our duties, or by what test we may know them; but no system of ethics requires that the sole motive of all we do shall be a feeling of duty..." (17). In this case, the rescuer passed the utilitarian test – he promoted the greatest happiness – and this is all we need to know.

2.2.3.1 Motive and the moral evaluation of conduct

In a famous footnote (18, fn. 2), Mill considers an objection to the above passage. The objector gives another rescue example that he argues can only be assessed as right or wrong by consideration of the motive with which the rescue was done.

> *Suppose that a tyrant, when his enemy jumped into the sea to escape from him, saved him from drowning simply in order that he might inflict upon him more exquisite tortures, would it tend to clearness to speak of that recue as a "morally right action"?*

The point of the example is to show first, that we would not speak of the rescue as a morally right action, and second, this is because the malevolent motive of the tyrant's act of rescue is not to save the man's life, but to torture him.

Mill's reply makes a distinction between two actions: the rescue and the torture, where the rescue is a *means* to the torture. Seen in this way, *"the rescue of the man is...only the necessary first step of an act far more atrocious than leaving him to drown would have been"* (18, fn. 2). If we consider the act *as a whole*, that is, as an act of torture, then we would certainly not speak of it as a "morally right action," and there is no need to consult the tyrant's motive to arrive at this assessment. An application of the principle of utility is all that we need to determine wrongdoing.

2.2.3.2 Motive and intention

Mill makes a second point. He writes that the objector "has confounded the very different ideas of Motive and Intention." The intention is "what the agent wills to do." The motive is "the feeling which makes him will so to do." The morality of the tyrant's act depends entirely upon the *intentional* act of torturing his enemy. This is what he "wills to do." The tyrant's motive, *whatever it may be*, makes no difference in estimating the morality of the act of torture

However, Mill writes, motive may make "a great difference in our moral estimation of the agent" (18, fn.2). Returning to Mill's original example, if it is asked "What makes it morally right to rescue the girl from drowning?" we would refer to a rule of conduct (e.g. utility) to answer the question. If it is also asked about the same person "Why do they call him a *bad* person?" we would answer by referring to his motive ("to collect a reward").

If a person causes harm to another unintentionally (by mistake or by accident), we would count this as an excuse and not hold her responsible. It is different with motive. If a poor person steals a loaf of bread from the baker and says that her motive was "To feed my child," the baker would still hold her responsible for the theft. A benevolent motive is not an excuse. If the baker considers the thief's motive at all, it would be to decide the amount of blame or reparation. In this case, given the thief's plea of poverty, the baker might decide to do nothing and let her keep the bread she stole.

2.2.4 *Utilitarians are frozen people*
It is said of utilitarianism that:

> ...it renders men cold and unsympathizing; that it chills their moral feelings toward individuals; that it makes them regard only the dry and hard consideration of the consequences of actions; not taking into their moral estimate the qualities from which those actions emanate.

Mill replies that this objection, like the last, misconceives the "purpose of a standard of morality and of the very meaning of the words 'right' and 'wrong'." The purpose of a moral standard is to help us decide whether an action is right or wrong. This is not decided by assessing the character of the person who did the act. We would not say of the person who rescues the drowning man that what he did is right or wrong because it is done by a good or bad man; "still less because it is done by an amiable, brave or benevolent man, or the contrary" (19).

It is one thing to morally evaluate an action or omission. It is quite another to evaluate persons. In the former case we look to a moral standard, whether that standard be utility or the categorical imperative. In the latter case, we look to past conduct, and to the motives that prompted the conduct. Martin Luther King is generally thought to be a good man, partly because of his tireless efforts to promote racial equality, and because his motive for this was a benevolent regard for the welfare of racial minorities.

2.2.5 *Utilitarianism is a godless doctrine*
The objection that utilitarianism is a godless doctrine can be interpreted in several ways. If God's purpose in creating human beings was that they achieve happiness, then "utility is not only not a godless doctrine, but more profoundly religious than any other" (21).

By "godless" the critic might mean that "utilitarianism does not recognize the revealed will of God as the supreme law of morals" (21). Mill replies that those utilitarians who also believe in the existence of God *necessarily believe* that His desire is for His human creations to always act to produce the greatest happiness. The utilitarian principle *must* be the "supreme law" of a God who is defined as "perfectly good and wise."

2.2.6 Expediency and acting on principle

The objectors to the utilitarian theory sometimes accuse it of being an "immoral doctrine" because it recommends doing what is expedient instead of acting on principle.

The objection itself is confusing because what the utilitarian recommends is that we adopt and act on the *principle* of utility as our rule and guide. Hence, the objector either has in mind some other principle than utility, or she interprets the utilitarian principle as one that justifies expedient behavior or policies.

If no other competing moral principle has been mentioned, then we can put the first alternative aside and concentrate on the second. Does the utilitarian justify expedient behavior or policies? The dictionary definition of "expedient" is "a means of attaining an end, especially one that is convenient but considered improper or immoral" (Cambridge). The question is whether the utilitarian principle could be used to justify improper or immoral means to attaining an end.

Mill uses the example of telling a lie "for the purpose of getting over some momentary embarrassment or attaining some object immediately useful to ourselves or others." But these purposes do not justify the lie. Lies may sometimes be useful for the person who tells the lie, but such lies are generally hurtful to others. They do this "by weakening the trustworthiness of human assertion" (22).

> Mill's warning about the damage that lies can make to the "trustworthiness of human assertion" is especially important to heed in the twenty-first century when a lie is not only rapidly transmitted to millions of people, but it is repeatedly told by some people who are in positions of authority.

This is not to deny that there may be exceptions to the rule that we ought to tell the truth, "sacred as it is." The withholding of the truth might be necessary to save others "from great and unmerited evil, and when the withholding can only be effected by the denial." Thus, it is justifiable on grounds of utility for a captured prisoner in time of war to withhold facts from the enemy which, if not withheld, could result in the death of hundreds of his fellow soldiers. "If the principle of utility is good for anything, it must be good for weighing these conflicting utilities against one another and marking out the region within which one or the other preponderates" (23).

2.2.7 The impracticality of the utility principle

The previous objections have been about alleged moral flaws in the utilitarian theory. The next objection is about its impracticality – "there is not time, previous to action, for calculating and weighing the effects of any line of conduct on the general happiness" (23). After all, the utilitarian principle requires us to predict the probable good and bad consequences of alternative lines of conduct. We must make this prediction about the future from what we know about the past. In the example at the beginning of the chapter, Maria breaks a promise to help Juan prepare for the upcoming philosophy examination. She did this because she needed to go home to help her ailing mother. We predicted that the outcome of a utility calculation would justify the broken promise. In her case, there may have been sufficient time to do the necessary calculation. But there are many other cases requiring careful calculations that we simply do not have time to do. For example, Ludwig is the single father of three small children. He is on the way to a job interview. He is currently jobless, living on money he borrows from friends. The job interview is at a location that requires him to take a short-cut on a road that is infrequently used. He comes upon an overturned car and notices that there are three elderly persons, all unconscious, inside the car. He sees smoke emanating from the engine. His cell phone does not have a signal. He can either turn back 20 miles to a place where he can get a signal and call for help, ignore the overturned car and continue to his destination, or he can stop his car and try to get the unconscious people out before the interior of the car catches fire.

Ludwig is a committed utilitarian, but he realizes that in this case, there is not time to make the requisite number of utility calculations, involving the balance of pleasure over pain that would be produced by each of several different choices. The *relevant* pleasures and pain to be calculated are those that would be experienced by himself, his children, the persons from whom he is borrowing money, the elderly people trapped in the car, and the persons waiting for him to show up for the interview. He must calculate the probability that these experiences would occur, as well as their intensity and duration, and all of this based on his knowledge of past cases.

There is simply no time to make complex utility calculations prior to taking any meaningful action. And if Ludwig takes the time, he risks losing the opportunity to get a good job *and* saving the lives of the elderly people in the car.

What should Ludwig do? It looks like the utilitarian theory itself has a serious flaw: *disutility*. It can't be effectively used in cases that require a quick decision. Should the theory be abandoned?

Mill comes to the rescue with the following reply:

> The answer to the objection is that there has been ample time, namely, the whole past duration of the human species. During all that time mankind have been learning by experience the tendencies of actions, on which experience all the prudence as well as all the morality of life are dependent...It is truly a whimsical supposition that, if mankind were agreed in considering utility to be the test of morality, they would remain without any agreement as to what is useful, and would take no measures for having their notions on

the subject taught to the young and enforced by law and opinion...Mankind must by this
time have acquired positive beliefs as to the effects of some actions on their happiness, and
the beliefs which have thus come down are the rules of morality for the multitude, and for
the philosopher until he has succeeded in finding better (23).

To put it simply, utilitarians can use ordinary moral rules when fast decisions must be made in an emergency. They can assume that the necessary utility calculations have been made long ago. These calculations are embodied in the rules of our everyday morality. In the case of Ludwig, he knows (by nurture, not nature) that he has moral obligations to his children, to the persons waiting to interview him, as well as to the elderly people trapped in a burning vehicle. He only has one more task. He must give precedence to one of these obligations. He might without hesitation run to the burning car and drag the unconscious people away to a safe place. This might cost him a job and perhaps disappoint his children and creditors, but he has decided that the obligation to save the life of another human being is a more important rule of morality (that is, it is higher in the scale of social utility) than the obligation to pay financial debts and to buy new clothes and toys for his children.

Mill refers to our everyday moral rules (e.g. "Tell the truth," "Keep your promises") as *corollaries* from the principle of utility. The corollaries are not absolute rules, having no exceptions. Like all practical rules, "they admit of indefinite improvement." The improvement can be seen in the exceptions. Thus, the moral rule that obliges us to tell the truth has an exception that says, "except when telling the truth would cause death or serious injury to another". For example, we are *not morally required* to tell the truth to a murderer at the door who asks us if we know the whereabouts of a friend who is hiding inside. We know from centuries of experience that an *absolute* imperative to tell the truth in circumstances like this will inevitably lead to more unhappiness than happiness.

> The example of the murderer at the door is from Immanuel Kant, who uses the example to argue for his view that "to be truthful (honest) in all declarations is, therefore, a sacred and unconditionally commanding law of reason that admits of no expediency whatsoever." (Kant, 63).

Mill sums up his position about the necessity of utility-based moral rules with this disparaging remark, undoubtedly aimed at those who, like Kant, subscribe to a "no exceptions" interpretation of moral rules (like telling the truth and keeping promises):

Whatever we adopt as the fundamental principle of morality, we require subordinate principles to apply it by; the impossibility of doing without them, being common to all systems, can afford no argument against any one in particular; but gravely to argue ... as if mankind had remained till now, and always must remain, without drawing any general conclusions from the experience of human life is as high a pitch, I think, as an absurdity has ever reached in philosophical controversy (24).

2.2.8 Utilitarianism provides people with an excuse for evil-doing

Mill concludes chapter II by reporting the following charge against the utilitarian:

We are told that a utilitarian will be apt to make his own particular case an exception to moral rules, and, when, under temptation, will see a utility in the breach of a rule, greater than he will see in its observance (24-25).

Mill has two responses. First, the accusation that people will interpret a moral rule in a way favorable to their own case is more a complaint about human nature than it is about utilitarianism or any other moral system.

There is no ethical creed which does not temper the rigidity of its laws by giving a certain latitude, under its moral responsibility of the agent for accommodation in particular circumstances and under every creed, at the opening thus made, self-deception and dishonest casuistry get in (25, my emphasis).

When accused with having done something morally wrong, it is the first instinct of many to defend themselves by denying either that they did not do what they are accused of doing or that the relevant moral rule does not apply in their case.

John Locke had made the same complaint about how people in the state of nature would understand and apply the natural law: "for though the law of nature be plain and intelligible by all rational creatures; yet men being biased by their interest, as well as ignorant for want of study of it, are not apt to allow of it as a law binding to them in the application of it to their particular case" (Locke, §124).

Second, every ethical theory must deal with "unequivocal cases of conflicting obligation" (25). Kant's example of the murderer at the door is only one of many examples. But this is where utilitarianism shines. If two moral obligations come into conflict, for example, "Tell the truth" and "Preserve and protect human life," then the principle of utility can be invoked to decide between them. It is only when there is no such appeal that we allow "a free scope for the action of personal desires and partialities" (25).

2.3 Summary and conclusion

The point of Mill's replies is to give the reader an accurate account of "what utilitarianism is." Here is a summary of what he has taught his readers about utilitarianism.

1) The pleasures of which human beings are capable are both mental and bodily.
    a) Mental pleasures are superior to bodily pleasures, when measured by either quantitative or qualitative standards.
    b) One pleasure is qualitatively superior to another only if all or almost all of those who have had experience of both prefer it.
2) When calculating the amount of pleasure and pain that might be caused by doing one action rather than another, the agent must *impartially* consider the pleasure and pain of *all persons affected* by each action, not just his own pleasure and pain.
3) The sacrifice of one's own happiness is "wasted" if it does not increase or tend to increase the sum total of happiness.
4) When deciding whether an action is right or wrong one should consider only whether the act produces the greatest happiness for the greatest number, *not* whether the agent is a good or bad person or whether the agent had a good or bad motive for doing the act.
5) When deciding whether an action is right or wrong, it is relevant to ask whether the agent *intentionally* brought about the consequence of the action (that is, whether the agent brought about the consequence by mistake or by accident).
6) Common moral rules like "tell the truth" and "keep your promises" can be used by a utilitarian to decide right and wrong, especially in those cases in which there is not time to do a thorough utility calculation.
    a) The utilitarian considers common moral rules to be "corollaries" of the principle of utility, meaning that they can be derived from the principle. Moral rules are summaries of the past effects of actions on human happiness.
    b) In situations where two rules of moral obligation come into conflict, the principle of utility can be invoked to settle the question.
    c)

2.4 Questions for thought and discussion

1. Some scholars have criticized Mill for importing a non-utilitarian standard when he declares that the mental pleasures are qualitatively superior to the bodily pleasures. Do you agree?

2. Of two mental pleasures, which one is superior: Watching the Super Bowl or listening to Rachmaninoff's Piano Concerto No. 3? Explain your choice.

3. Of two lives, which one is superior: the life of a dissatisfied genius or the life of a satisfied moron?

4. Suppose that the bakery store thief (referred to at 2.2.3.2) says "What I did was not morally wrong because I did it to feed my child. I have a stronger obligation to care for my child than my obligation to refrain from theft." Is this a counter-example to Mill's claim that motive has nothing to do with decisions about whether an action is right or wrong?

5. Why does Mill think it important to consider intention but not motive as an important element in utilitarian decisions about right and wrong

6. We are told that utilitarians must not only consider the short-term consequences of their conduct, but they must also calculate all the probable long-term consequences. Does this make the utility principle useless in moral decision-making? Is there a remedy?

7. Is utilitarianism a "godless doctrine"?

References

Bentham, Jeremy. 2003. Bentham on push-pin vs. poetry. (from *The Rationale of Reward*). Ed. Troyer, John. *The Classical Utilitarians: Bentham and Mill*. Indianapolis: Hackett.

Kant, Immanuel. 1785. *Groundwork of the Metaphysics of Morals*. Trans. Thomas Kingsmill Abbott. https://en.wikisource.org/wiki/Groundwork_of_the_Metaphysics_of_Morals

Locke, John. 1980 [1690]. *Second Treatise of Government*. Ed. C.B. Macpherson. Indianapolis: Hackett.

Oxford English Dictionary. 2018. London: Oxford University Press.

Plato. c. 390 BCE. *Republic*. https://en.wikipedia.org/wiki/Republic_(Plato)

Chapter 3 The Ultimate Sanction (*Utilitarianism* III)

Although the motive of a person has nothing to do with whether his conduct is morally right or wrong, it has much to do with the **sanction** of a foundational moral principle, including the principle of utility. What are the motives to obey a principle that says we must always do the *optimific* act? How does the utilitarian principle get its "binding force" on those who adopt it? What are the sanctions for *not* obeying the principle of utility? In general, *why should I be moral?*

3.1 The sanctions which belong to any system of morals

Questions about sanctions arise for any system of morals. All ethical theories must explain why we should feel obliged to do the actions commanded by their foundational principle. Thus, Locke must provide us with a motive for obeying the law of nature; Kant must explain why we are obliged to conform our conduct to the categorical imperative; and Mill must show us the sanctions for failing to promote the greatest happiness for the greatest number.

The two kinds of sanctions that apply to all ethical theories are *external* and *internal*.

3.1.1 External sanctions

By an external sanction or motive Mill means

> ...the hope of favor and the fear of displeasure from our fellow creatures or from the
> Ruler of the universe, along with whatever we may have of sympathy or affection for them,
> or of love and awe of Him, inclining us to do His will independently of selfish consequences
> (27).

If you do not want your friends, family, business associates, or God to dislike you, then your fear of this dislike will serve as a strong motive for conforming your conduct to any system of morals, including utilitarianism. If you want their favor, then this also will serve as a motive for obedience.

Mill insists that there is no reason why these motives "should not attach themselves to the utilitarian morality as completely and as powerfully as to any other" (27). Mill goes further than this by reminding us that "men do desire happiness," and any moral principle that emphasizes their own happiness and any conduct of others that promotes their happiness will certainly give them a strong inducement toward the utilitarian principle.

"With regard to the religious motive," Mill observes that this is no impediment to utilitarianism. "Those who think that conduciveness to the general happiness is the essence or even only the criterion of good must necessarily believe that it is also that which God approves" (27). In other words, God is a utilitarian. You cannot find a better external motive for adopting the utilitarian morality than that!

This reply reverses the Divine Command Theory which says that an act is morally obligatory only if it is commanded by the deity, implying that there are no rational restraints on God's commands. Mill asserts that God only commands acts that are obligatory, and it is conduciveness to the general happiness that makes them obligatory.

3.1.2 Internal sanctions

As Plato often stressed in *Republic* and other dialogues, the external motives for moral behavior do not guarantee that people will always do the morally right act or refrain from wrongful conduct. The favor of others motivates the bad person to maintain a good reputation, not necessarily to do what is morally right. There are bad people who know how to "game the system." They manage to maintain a good reputation because they know how to lie, cheat and steal without ever being found out (*Republic*, 362c).

Mill proposes another motive for being moral, a motive that will have a stronger prohibitive effect on a person who contemplates wrongdoing. He suggests that the motive we seek is to be found internally, in ourselves. It is commonly called "conscience."

Mill defines "conscience" as:

> ...a feeling in our own mind; a pain, more or less intense, attendant on violation of duty, which in properly cultivated moral natures, rises, in the more serious cases, into shrinking from it as an impossibility (27).

This is what is lacking in the person who is only taught that being moral is a means to keeping a good reputation in the community. If he does not have a conscience to restrain him, then he will violate a moral duty whenever he can safely get away with this. There is little or no internal pain he feels when contemplating a future wrongful deed.

Conscience is a *prospective moral feeling*, that is, it is what we feel *before* we violate a rule of right conduct. Remorse and guilt are *retrospective*. They are feelings we must encounter *after* the violation.

Mill refers to conscience as the "ultimate sanction of *all* morality" (28). Hence, the feeling of conscience is the sanction of the utilitarian moral standard, there being no reason why this feeling "may not be cultivated to as great intensity in connection with the utilitarian as with any other rule of morals" 28).

Plato does not refer to "conscience" or "remorse" as ultimate sanctions in his dialogues, although his discussion of the "just soul" shows that it might serve the same purpose. A person has a just soul when each part of the soul (appetite, emotion, reason) is doing the work it is naturally suited to do, with the element of "reason" having supremacy (Republic, 443b). This is the healthiest condition of the soul, and (it is argued) the person who cultivates this condition would never commit immoral acts such as betrayal of a friend, untrustworthiness, temple robbery, adultery, disrespecting parents, or neglecting the gods (442d-e).

3.2 Utilitarianism, conscience and the social feelings of mankind

Is it possible for feelings of conscience and remorse to attach themselves to the utilitarian principle?

Perhaps we should first ask "What kind of question is this?" Is it a scientific question, answered empirically, with reference to observation and experience, or is it a philosophical question, answered analytically, with reference to relevant concepts and their interrelationships?

Perhaps the best way to answer is to look at Mill's methodology. Here is his argument for the conclusion that conscientious feelings (conscience) can and do serve as a sanction for the utilitarian standard.

1. Conscientious feelings (conscience) can firmly attach to the utilitarian standard only if there is a natural sentiment for the utilitarian morality.

2. There is a natural sentiment for the utilitarian morality, namely the social feelings of mankind (the desire to be in unity with our fellow creatures).

3. Therefore, conscientious feelings can firmly attach to the utilitarian standard.

The argument is deductive, and it is valid, that is, if we accept the premises as true, then the conclusion must be true.

But are the premises true? In premises 1 and 2, the term *natural sentiment* is a concept often used in the nineteenth century to express the view that *morality* is based on a sentiment or feeling that is part of our natural makeup (Oxford Reference). This does not mean that the feeling is innate, nor does it mean that everyone has these feelings. Mill believes that it is acquired in the same way that speaking and reasoning are acquired. And like speaking and reasoning, children can develop it to a high degree by careful parental attention and cultivation. Others will develop it to a lesser degree, and still others do not develop it at all.

In premise 2, Mill gives a name to the natural sentiment. It is "the *social feelings* of mankind--the desire to be in unity with our fellow creatures" (30). This is reminiscent of Aristotle, who famously wrote:

> Man is by nature a social animal; an individual who is unsocial naturally and not accidentally is either beneath our notice or more than human. Society is something that precedes the individual. Anyone who either cannot lead the common life or is so self-sufficient as not to need to, and therefore does not partake of society, is either a beast or a god (*Politics* II (9) 1253a)

Mill goes somewhat farther than Aristotle by writing not just that humans are "social," but that they have "social *feelings*, the *desire* to be in unity with our fellow creatures." Mill agrees with Aristotle that humans are beings who naturally "partake of society." He adds to this the observation that after a relatively short period, humans will begin to have "a temporary feeling that the interests of others are their own interests" (31). That feeling, with proper cultivation, soon becomes permanent:

> Not only does all strengthening of social ties, and all healthy growth of society, give to each individual a stronger personal interest in practically consulting the welfare of others, it also leads him to identify his feelings more and more with their good, or at least with an even greater degree of practical consideration for it. He comes, as though instinctively, to be conscious of himself as a being who of course pays regard to others. The good of others becomes to him a thing naturally and necessarily to be attended to, like any of the physical conditions of our existence (31).

This is clearly an *empirical claim* about human nature. However, social psychologists in the twentieth century cite obvious counter-examples that falsify the idea that humans are naturally oriented toward each other in the ways suggested by Aristotle and Mill.

> We engage in acts of loyalty, moral concern, and cooperation primarily toward our inner circles, but do so at the expense of people outside of those circles. Our altruism is not unbounded; it is parochial. In support of this phenomenon, the hormone oxytocin, long considered to play a key role in forming social bonds, has been shown to facilitate affiliation toward one's ingroup, but can increase defensive aggression toward one's outgroup. Other research suggests that this self-sacrificial intragroup love co-evolved with intergroup war, and that societies who most value loyalty to each other tend to be those most likely to endorse violence toward outgroups (Waytz).

By extension, social psychologists would also disagree with Mill that the desire to be in unity with our fellow creatures is something we naturally feel toward *all* humans, no matter what we know about their race, ethnicity, social class or religion. In fairness to Mill, he does point out that our moral feelings are susceptible "of being cultivated in almost any direction." If they are cultivated to favor one's ingroup, it is still the case that people *in these groups* will have social feelings for one another, even if they are weaker or nonexistent for those who are in outgroups.

If we agree to the limited claim that humans naturally have social feelings only *for persons in their ingroup*, then it *does not follow* that conscience is or can be "the ultimate sanction of the greatest happiness morality" (33). That is, the conclusion (3) of the preceding argument does not follow from the premises because *there is no natural sentiment* for the utilitarian morality. The utilitarian principle requires us to promote the greatest happiness for the *greatest number*, not the greatest happiness *for the people in my ingroup*. The internal sanction of conscience may act as "a powerful binding force," but it only binds us to promote the interests of people in our inner circle, not those outside the circle.

This does not mean that the desire to be in unity with our fellow creatures cannot ever extend to a desire to be in unity with all humans. It means only that this desire does not *naturally* so extend. If it does extend to outgroups, it does so by education. *You have got to be taught* to identify your feelings with the good of those outside your ingroup as much as you identify your feelings with the good of those in your circle.

> Compare the findings of social psychology about the origin of moral feelings with the second and third stanzas of the song "You've Got to be Carefully Taught," from the Rodgers and Hammerstein musical South Pacific:
>
> You've got to be taught to be afraid
> Of people whose eyes are oddly made
> And people whose skin is a different shade
> You've got to be carefully taught
>
> You've got to be taught before it's too late
> Before you are six or seven or eight
> To hate all the people your relatives hate
> You've to be carefully taught

3.3 Questions for thought and discussion

1. Why should you be moral? Suppose you come across a man's wallet lying on the sidewalk. You pick it up and find over one hundred dollars and several credit cards, as well as a driver's license identifying the owner of the wallet. No one has seen you pick up the wallet. You can remove the money and credit cards and discard the wallet in a nearby trashcan, without anyone noticing. If returning the wallet to its rightful

owner is the morally right thing to do, what are the sanctions (motives) for not returning the wallet? Can the utilitarian claim the same motives?

2. What is the difference between feeling guilty and feeling ashamed? How do these moral feelings function as motives or sanctions for the utilitarian moralist?

3. Plato's answer to the question "Why should I be moral?" is that it is in our own psychological self-interest that we should conform our conduct to ordinary moral rules (3.1.2). Those who are "completely unjust" will suffer greatly by allowing the worst part of the soul to dominate their life. Does Mill give a more plausible answer to this question?

4. Mill says that ordinary moral rules like "Keep your promises," and "Tell the truth" are corollaries of the principle of utility. If I feel remorse about breaking a promise or telling a lie, does this show that I also feel remorse about violating the principle of utility? How can a moral feeling (like remorse) attach itself to the utilitarian principle if most people know nothing about the principle?

References

Aristotle. c. 350 BCE. *Politics*. University of Chicago.

Oxford Dictionary of English. 2018. Ed. Angus Stevenson. London: Oxford University Press.

Sorabji, Richard. 2014. *Moral Conscience through the Ages: Fifth Century BCE to the Present*. University of Chicago Press.

Waytz, Adam. What scientific ideas are ready for retirement? Humans are by nature social animals. 2014. https://www.edge.org/response-detail/25395

Chapter 4 Proof of the Principle of Utility (*Utilitarianism* IV)

Mill previously stated (2.1) that the utilitarian principle has a theory of life as its foundation. The theory has two elements: (1) Happiness is desirable as an end; and (2) Happiness is the only thing desirable as an end.

Mill's task in this chapter is to prove both elements and to link them to a final proof of the principle of utility.

4.1 A proof that happiness is desirable as an end

In chapter I Mill had said that "questions of ultimate ends do not admit of proof." He meant that a question about whether an ultimate end is good cannot be proved by "reasoning." If an end is "ultimate," then *by definition*, it cannot be proved (reasoned) to be good on the ground that it is a means to something else that is good.

But Mill also said in chapter I that "there is a larger meaning of the word 'proof'" in which "considerations may be presented capable of determining the intellect either to give or withhold its assent to the doctrine, and this is equivalent to proof." (5) Mill will now tell us something about these "considerations."

> ...questions of ultimate ends..., being matters of fact, may be the subject of a direct appeal to the faculties which judge of fact—namely, our senses and the internal consciousness (34).

For example, we use the faculty of sight to prove that an object is visible. We use the faculty of hearing to prove that a sound is audible. "In like manner, I apprehend, the sole evidence it is possible to produce that anything is desirable is that people actually desire it" (34).

This is the promised "consideration" which Mill earlier claimed (1.4) will convince us to give our assent to the doctrine that happiness is desirable as an end.

> No reason can be given why the general happiness is desirable, except that each person, so far as he believes it to be attainable, desires his own happiness. This, however, being a fact, we have not only all the proof which the case admits of, but all which it is possible to require, that happiness is a good, that each person's happiness is a good to that person, and the general happiness, therefore, a good to the aggregate of all persons. Happiness has made out its title as one of the ends of conduct and, consequently, one of the criteria of morality (34).

Let's back up a bit and look at the analogy between the faculties of sight and hearing and the faculty of desire. Here is how the analogy figures in an inductive argument:

1. The only proof it is possible to require that an object is visible or audible is that people see it or hear it.

2. The desirability of happiness is analogous to the visibility or audibility of an object.

3. Therefore, the only proof it is possible to require that happiness is desirable is that people desire it.

The flaw in this argument is premise #2. There is no exact analogy between "desirability" and "visibility" or "audibility." To say that something is visible or audible is to say that it *can be seen* or *can be heard*. But this is not what is meant when we say that something is desirable. If I say that a feeling (e.g. pleasure) is desirable, I am *not* saying that "The feeling of pleasure can be desired." Instead, I am *evaluating the feeling as good*. If we are in the grocery store looking for apples to purchase and I say to you "that one looks desirable," I do not mean that *it is possible* for you to desire it. I mean "That is a good one; you should choose it" (G.E. Moore refers to this as "the naturalistic fallacy" 118.).

Although the analogy between "desirable" and "visible" is flawed, Mill might take another tack. He might say that he is recommending a *standard for grading feelings* as more or less good or desirable. The standard would involve taking a simple poll of people who have experienced the feeling. The question for them is "Do you desire this feeling?" If a majority of people answer in the affirmative, then the feeling is graded as desirable (good). If the majority is over (say) ninety percent, then it is graded as "highly desirable" (very good or excellent).

When asked about the feeling of happiness (pleasure and the absence of pain), it is probable that a large majority of people who have experienced happiness would give it the highest grade. When asked about the feeling of unhappiness (pain and the privation of pleasure), it is probable that the same majority would give it the lowest grade ("highly undesirable" or "very bad").

However, there are alternative standards for grading happiness or pleasure. Mill has previously said that he wants to evaluate pleasures by the competence of those are experiencing them. "Of two pleasures if there be one to which all or almost all *who have experience of both* give a decided preference ...that is the *more desirable* pleasure." (8). Other standards would use measurable ranking factors such as intensity and duration (Bentham).

This might complicate the simple poll outlined above. To prove that happiness is desirable, it will now be necessary to accommodate those who insist on knowing the *kind* of pleasure before they will tell us whether or not they desire it. After all, we have been told by Mill that those who are "completely acquainted" with both the mental and the physical pleasures "give a decided preference" to the mental pleasures. There are some people in this group who might go further than this and deny that they have *any* desire for some of the physical pleasures, for example sexual pleasure or the pleasure of mind-altering drugs.

Does this requirement skew the grading results of the poll? If it is true that some people in the polled group do not prefer some of the pleasures that are desired by others, then the standard used for grading happiness is altered as follows: Happiness is desirable only if those people *competently acquainted with both mental and physical pleasure* actually prefer it.

Notice, however, that this does not change Mill's general conclusion in #3 that happiness is desirable because it is desired. Restricting the members of the group who are polled does not change the conclusion. Those who desire happiness will grade it as desirable, even though they might grade some pleasures as less desirable than the grade given it by others. It is still true that happiness is desirable because it is desired, regardless of whether the desire is mental or physical.

4.2 A proof that happiness is the only thing desirable as an end

The only thing proved in 4.1 is that happiness is *one* of the things desirable as an end. Mill has yet to prove that it is the *only* thing desirable as an end.

If happiness is the only thing desirable as an end, then *everything else* that we call desirable (good) is desirable because it is a *means* to happiness.

Is there anything besides happiness that might be a candidate for "the ultimate end of human action"? The traditional reply to this question is "virtue and the absence of vice." There are people who desire virtue "no less really than pleasure and the absence of pain."

> *And hence the opponents of the utilitarian standard deem that they have a right to infer that there are other ends of human action besides happiness, and that happiness is not the standard of approbation and disapprobation* (33)

Aristotle might have been an opponent had he lived in the mid-nineteenth century and Mill *might* have dismissed his claim that virtue is an end of human action with the remark that virtue is desired only because it is a means to happiness. It is not an end in itself. But he surprises us with this lengthy remark:

> *The utilitarian doctrine...maintains not only that virtue is to be desired, but that it is to be desired disinterestedly, for itself...They not only place virtue at the very head of the things which are good as means to the ultimate end but they also recognize as a psychological fact the possibility of its being, to the individual, a good in itself, without*

looking to any end beyond it, and hold that the mind is not in a right state, not in a state conformable to utility, not in the state most conducive to the general happiness, unless it does love virtue in this manner, as a thing desirable in itself.

How can Mill hold both of the following positions? (1) Happiness is the only thing desirable as an end; and (2) Virtue is a good in itself, without looking to any end beyond it. If happiness is the only thing is desirable as an end, then it follows that there is *nothing else, including virtue*, that is also desirable as an end. To put it bluntly, (2) contradicts (1).

4.2.1 Parts (ingredients) of happiness

Mill responds that he has not departed from the happiness principle – because *there is no contradiction* in holding both (1) and (2). Here is how he pulls off this hat trick. First, he claims that happiness has "ingredients" or "parts." Second, the love of virtue, for some people can become a part of their conception of happiness.

Although virtue is "naturally and originally" a means to happiness it is capable of becoming so; and in those who live it disinterestedly, it has become so, and it is desired and cherished, not as a means to happiness, but as a part of their happiness (34).

Mill illustrates the process of how a desire for something starts out as *a means* to one's conception of happiness, and eventually becomes *a part* of that conception. His example is the love of money. "There is nothing originally more desirable about money than about any heap of littering pebbles." We desire money because of the things which money will buy: food, clothes, shelter. Money is a means to these ends. But at least for some people the desire to possess money at some point in their lives becomes stronger than the desire to use. "It may, then, be said truly that money is desired not for the sake of an end, but as part of the end. From being a means to happiness, it has come to be itself a principle ingredient of the individual's conception of happiness" (34)

Richard Walters, a homeless man who lived in Phoenix, died in 2009. He left behind a $4 million estate (National Public Radio). A homeless woman who was living out of a shopping cart died on the streets of Manhattan in the same year. She had secretly amassed nearly $300,000 (Amira). A homeless man in Skellefteå, Sweden spent his days collecting tin cans. Most people avoided him because he smelled bad and had a general lack of hygiene. In 2010, 8 months after dying of a heart attack at the age of 60, his relatives discovered that he had left a fortune of 1.66 million dollars (Noone).

The cases illustrate Mill's point. These people became psychologically incapable of spending the money they had accumulated. Over time, the love of money became for them an end-in-itself, not a means to happiness.

Mill gives two other examples: fame and power. Think of the aging actress who is severely depressed because she is no longer famous or the deposed dictator who lives in exile in a luxurious palace but lapses into depression because he can no longer wield political power. The fame of the actress and the power of the dictator which were originally a means to happiness became at some point part of their very conception of happiness. It was so deeply a part of their conception of happiness that they could not be happy without the fame or the power.

4.2.2 Virtue as a part of happiness

A part or ingredient of happiness is not like a part or ingredient of an automobile or a pie. It is not a tangible object. It is a *psychologically* necessary condition for happiness. It is a desire for something which if not satisfied prevents the person from being happy. This especially applies to the desire of virtue.

> Virtue, according to the utilitarian conception, is a good of this description. There was no original desire of it, or motive to it, save the conduciveness to pleasure, and especially to protection from pain. But through the association thus formed it may be felt good in itself, and desired as such with as great intensity as any other good (37).

The important difference between the love of virtue and the love of money, power and fame, is that the latter three desires can lead to harmful consequences, the lust for money and power being the two which can do the most damage to others. But *the love of virtue can never be harmful to others.* It can be cultivated "up to the greatest strength as possible," without causing harm to anyone. Indeed, the very reverse is true. Those who love virtue can only promote the general happiness (37).

Mill summarizes the argument in the following quote:

> It results from the preceding considerations that there is in reality nothing desired except happiness. Whatever is desired otherwise than as a means to some end beyond itself, and ultimately to happiness, is desired as itself a part of happiness, and is not desired for itself until it has become so (37).

4.3 Proof of the utility principle in argument form

Mill begins the final proof of the principle of utility with a hypothetical about human psychology.

1. "If human nature is so constituted as to desire nothing which is not either a part of happiness or a means of happiness—we can have no other proof, and we require no other—that these are the only things desirable."

Mill next adds the following empirical observation:

2. "Mankind do[es] desire nothing for itself but that which is a pleasure to them, or of which the absence is a pain."

If we combine #1 with #2, we can infer the following:

3. Therefore, the only things desirable (good) are those which are either a part of happiness or a means to happiness ("happiness is the sole end of human action").

Mill makes the following hidden assumption, which accordingly is put in brackets:

[4. Only the desirable and undesirable *consequences* of an act can be used to determine whether it is right or wrong.]

And he gets the conclusion:

5. Therefore, *"the promotion of happiness is the test by which to judge of all human conduct"* (38).

There are two unproved premises in this argument: #2 and #4. Mill immediately offers a proof of #2 but puts off any discussion of #4 until the next chapter (5.6). Let's take a careful look at #2.

4.3.1 Fact and experience or logical impossibility?

Mill writes that to decide whether it is really true that "mankind desire nothing for itself but that which is a pleasure to them, or of which the absence is a pain...is question of fact or experience." It is an empirical question that can only be answered by evidence. The evidence is gathered from self-observation and the observation of others. If I look within myself I will find that the things which are a pleasure to me are the same things that I desire, and the things I desire are the things that are also a pleasure.

Mill now goes a bit further by declaring that the words "desire" and "pleasure" are "two different modes of naming the same psychological fact." Mill concludes from this brief discussion that "to desire anything in proportion as the idea of it is pleasant is a physical and metaphysical impossibility" (38).

I would only point out that if it is a metaphysical impossibility for mankind to desire something which is not a pleasure to them, then there is no point in looking for evidence to the contrary. If I point to the masochist as an example of someone who desires pain, this would be rejected by claiming that it is not metaphysically possible to desire pain – because the masochist is using the pain as a *means* to pleasure. Mill *guarantees* the conclusion that no one desires pain as an end in itself by making it logically impossible to falsify it.

4.3.2 Only the desirable and undesirable consequences of an act can be used to determine right and wrong

The assumption in premise #4 might be true, but it clearly needs an argument for support. We won't get to this until the next chapter 5. But we can mention two deontological ethical theories that are strongly opposed: the theory of natural law (John Locke) and Kant's theory of the categorical imperative. According to Locke, a violation of the natural law is sufficient to conclude that the conduct is morally wrong. For example, if I kill one child to save the lives of five children, this is morally wrong even if it can be calculated that saving the lives of five children would produce much more happiness than unhappiness than would be produced by not killing the one child.

According to Kant, as discussed in chapter 1, the obligation not to make a false promise is absolute. It is morally wrong to make a false promise no matter what the circumstances, including the circumstance that the false promise might have overall good consequences by producing the greatest happiness for the greatest number.

4.4 Desire and will

The final objection to the utilitarian theory of life in this chapter is that "a person of confirmed virtue" will intentionally carry out his virtuous purposes without any thought of the pleasure he expects to derive from fulfilling these purposes. The purpose may become habitual, "and instead of willing the thing because we desire it, we often desire it only because we will it" (38-39). Here is an example. Suppose you are taught at an early age that it is desirable to open the windows in your bedroom at night in order to let in the fresh outside air. For the first year you willed (intended) to open the window because you wanted it opened (you desired this outcome). But this purpose became habitual. Even when the outside temperature dropped below freezing, you never gave a thought about what you were doing as you opened the windows. If asked whether you wanted to open the windows, you might respond "I desired it but only in the sense that I intentionally opened the window—but certainly not with the intent of letting in freezing air."

Isn't this a serious objection to the utilitarian theory that happiness is the only thing good or desirable for itself? Mill's reply is that "will is the child of desire and passes out of the dominion of its parent only to come under that of habit" (39). Your intention (will) to open the window was originally driven by your desire to open it, but this intention (will) later become a habit. The same thing can and does happen to virtue. We are initially driven by desire to become virtuous, but this intention becomes habitual over time. This is a good thing, not only for the virtuous person but for all those who come into contact with him or her. Habit imposes certainty about what this person will do under a variety of moral challenges. We can count on what the virtuous person will do when it comes time to meet these challenges. This is why the utilitarian would encourage the cultivation of the will to do what is right as a habit in all of us and therefore, as another means to promote the greatest good for all.

4.5 Questions for thought and discussion

1. Mill does not say that he will give a direct proof that happiness is desirable. He will only give us considerations that will lead us to agree that happiness is desirable. What does he mean by a "direct proof"? What does he mean by "considerations"?

2. What are Mill's considerations that are supposed to get us to agree that happiness is desirable? Are you convinced? Explain.

3. How does Mill prove that happiness is the *only* thing desirable as an end? Can you think of any other candidates? Virtue? Courage? Moderation? Wisdom? Justice?

4. Why does Mill reject virtue as something that is desirable as an end?

5. What does Mill mean by "parts of happiness"? How do parts of happiness differ from means to happiness? Give a few examples.

6. What is the distinction between desire and will? How does this distinction affect the criticism that there are some people who always pursue the virtuous life even though they never give a thought to the pleasure of doing what is right and avoiding what is wrong?

References

Adkins, A.W.H. 1972. *Moral Values and Political Behaviour in Ancient Greece from Homer to the End of the Fifth Century*. London: Chatto and Windus.

Amira, Dan. 2009. Some homeless people are secretly wealthy. *New York Magazine: Daily Intelligencer*.
http://nymag.com/daily/intelligencer/2009/08/some_homeless_people_are_secre.html

Aristotle. c.350 BCE. *Nicomachean Ethics*.

Moore, G.E., 1993. *Principia Ethica*. Cambridge: Cambridge University Press.

National Public Radio. 2009. Homeless man leaves behind surprise 4 million. *Heard on All Things Considered.* https://www.npr.org/2009/07/27/.../homeless-man-leaves-behind-surprise-4-million

Noone, Lydia. 2010. Tin can collector dies a millionaire – what's his secret? *New York Daily News.* http://www.nydailynews.com/news/money/tin-collector-dies-millionaire-secret-article-1.164965

Chapter 5 The Connection Between Justice and Utility (*Utilitarianism* V)

Utilitarianism meets its most important challenge in this chapter. Unlike the several criticisms of the theory discussed in chapter II, the challenges in chapter V are *moral*. In chapter II, Mill answered criticisms that were based on mistaken interpretations of the utilitarian theory. In this chapter, however, the criticism is that utilitarianism would have us approve of actions that are *morally unacceptable*. The utilitarian theory, opponents say, justifies conduct that is *unjust* or a violation of fundamental moral rights. Any ethical theory that would justify such conduct should be discarded on the trash heap of failed philosophical speculation.

Mill takes the criticism very seriously. To make it easier to follow Mill's lengthy defense of the utilitarian theory, this chapter is broken down into several short sections.

5.1 Injustice and the feeling of injustice

Whether we believe that feelings of injustice are natural or instinctual, most of us are familiar with the way we react to situations in which we believe that an injustice has been done. If a woman is refused promotions that are regularly given to the men with whom she works, many of us upon hearing about this get upset or are outraged by the injustice of giving promotions based on gender. But Mill cautions that the fact that there are such emotional responses should not lead us to conclude that these feelings of injustice correspond to an independent moral principle.

> ...it is one thing to believe that we have natural feelings of justice, and another to acknowledge them as the ultimate criterion of conduct... Mankind are always predisposed to believe that any subjective feeling, not otherwise accounted for, is a revelation of some objective reality. (41)

You are at the zoo and you see a Bengal tiger. You might turn to your friend and say, "That tiger is terrifying." You are reporting your own subjective feelings about the tiger, not an objective feature that the tiger possesses. You observe (see) that the tiger is quite large, has sharp teeth, a light orange coat, with black stripes and a white belly. You do not see an additional feature called "terrifying."

By analogy, if you have a strong feeling of injustice when you witness an unarmed man being shot in the back by the police, you see *the act* of the man being shot by the police, but you do not see an *unjust act*. Instead, you use a "criterion of conduct" to *infer* the injustice of the act from an application of that criterion to what you have witnessed.

The philosophical question that Mill asks is whether the subjective feelings of justice and injustice, which are admittedly much stronger than the feelings which attach to simple expediency, "require a totally different origin." Is there a moral principle, independent of utility, that both supports the inference and explains your feelings of injustice in the gender discrimination example and the police shooting case? As Mill puts it, does justice "have an existence in nature as something absolute, generically distinct from every variety of the expedient, and, in idea, opposed to it?" (41). Is justice the name for an absolute moral rule or "criterion of conduct" that exists independently of the principle of utility, and which requires conduct that is a higher obligation than an obligation to promote the greatest good?

5.2 Modes of conduct considered to be unjust

The first step toward answering these questions is to define the term "unjust". To accomplish this, Mill takes a page from Socrates' dialogues and writes that the best way to find a definition is to identify several situations in which we use the word "unjust" and then ask what these situations have in common.

First, let's look at the six situations of injustice Mill identifies.

- *Violating the legal rights of anyone.*

  For example, you host a philosophy club party at your house. During the party someone enters your bedroom and goes through the dresser drawer where you keep your wallet and car keys. He steals both and drives away in your car.

- *Taking or withholding from any person that to which he/she has a moral right.*

  For example, miscegenation laws prohibiting interracial marriage in several states of the U.S.A. were not struck down by the U.S. Supreme Court until 1976. During the years before the Supreme Court decision, there were many people of different races who believed they had a moral right to marry, even though they had no legal right to do so.

- *Obtaining a good or undergoing an evil which one does not deserve.*

  For example, being awarded a scholarship even though you did not meet the minimum qualifications; getting a failing grade in a class because you refused to date the professor's daughter. In both cases, we would not hesitate to say that an injustice has been done.

- *Breaking faith with anyone (violating an engagement or disappointing expectations raised by your own conduct).*

For example, you break a promise to help a classmate study for the final exam, or you did not show up at her apartment even though earlier in the day you led her to believe that you were going to help her.

- *Being partial—showing favor or preference to one person over another in matters to which favor or preference do not apply.*

  For example, a judge in a court of law refuses to recuse herself from the case which she is deciding, even though it involves a lawsuit brought by a stranger against her favorite cousin.

- *Equality—treating like cases alike and different cases differently, provided that the likenesses and the differences are relevant.*

  For example, we would deem it *unjust* to (a) treat persons the same although they are relevantly different and (b) treat persons differently although they are relevantly alike. For example, two students, Gertrude and Edgar have the same scores on all exams, quizzes and lab work in their Physics class, but at the end of the term Edgar is awarded an "A" and Gertrude gets a "B".

Mill now surveys these uses of the term "injustice" and wonders about the "mental link" that holds them together. What do these cases have in common?

Mill answers the question by taking a hint from the etymology of the word (although he warns us not to assume that "a word must still continue to mean what it originally meant" [46]). He finds that the primitive origin of the word "justice" is "conformity to law" (46). Returning to the six examples of the ordinary language use of the word "unjust," Mill argues that what they have in common is that they all involve a *breach of law*, where "law" has a broad meaning that includes any kind of rule or command, legal or moral, that is backed with a sanction:

> When we think that a person is bound in justice to do a thing, it is an ordinary form of language to say that he ought to be compelled to do it. We should be gratified to see the obligation enforced by anybody who had the power (47, my emphasis).

5.3 The difference between morality and expediency

The preceding definition of "unjust" does not take us very far. The idea of a violation of law that is backed with a sanction is also built into the notion of any kind of wrongdoing. If you say of anyone, friend or foe, that they have done something you believe to be wrong, then depending on whether the wrongdoing is legal or moral, you imply either that they should be punished, ostracized, verbally condemned or at a minimum, feel and express remorse for what they did.

We do not call anything wrong unless we mean to imply that a person ought to be punished in some way or other for doing it—if not by law, by the opinion of his fellow creatures; if not by opinion, by the reproaches of his own conscience (47).

Both wrongdoing and acts of injustice can be distinguished from *imprudent acts* for this reason, that the wrongdoer and the unjust person have done what they are morally bound not to do. They are "proper objects of punishment." By way of contrast, persons who do something imprudent (for example, amateur rock climbing without a safety line) are doing something we wish they would not do, but they have no moral obligation to refrain from doing. Nor do we think they should they be punished for failing to change their behavior.

In his essay On Liberty, Mill makes a distinction between other-regarding and self-regarding acts. The former are acts that cause harm to others. The latter are acts that only cause harm to oneself. Acts of wrongdoing, including unjust acts, belong in the other-regarding class, and imprudent acts are self-regarding. Mill uses the distinction to determine what acts are justifiably punishable by law (and by public opinion).

5.4 The difference between justice and other branches of morality

If injustice is a type of wrongdoing, then what is it that distinguishes it from other types? Mill answers this question by borrowing a distinction from the ethical theory playbook:

...ethical writers divide moral duties into two classes, denoted by the ill-chosen expressions, duties of perfect and of imperfect obligation; the latter being those in which, though the act is obligatory, the particular occasions of performing it are left to our choice, as in the case of charity or beneficence, which we are indeed bound to practice but not toward any definite person nor at any prescribed time. In the more precise language of philosophic jurists, duties of perfect obligation are those duties in virtue of which a correlative right resides in some person or persons; duties of imperfect obligation are those moral obligations which do not give birth to any right (48).

For example, we have an imperfect obligation to give help to others when help is needed, but we are not morally required to do this for a specific person nor at any specific time. The charities to whom I give annual donations do not tell me that they have a right to the money I send to them. It is otherwise with duties of perfect obligation, for example, the duty not to kill one another. We have a ***prima facie*** duty because there is a correlative right (to life) possessed by *all* persons *all the time*. We cannot choose the persons to whom it applies, nor can we choose the time that it applies.

Mill writes that this feature is exactly the distinction between justice and other forms of morality.

> *Justice implies something which it is not only right to do, and wrong not to do, but which some individual person can claim from us as his moral right* (49).

When we say that an action is unjust we imply that a right has been violated. In the six examples spelled out in section 5.4, there is an implication that a wrong has been done, a right has been violated "and some assignable person who is wronged" (49). When I say that it is unjust for someone to have taken my wallet, car keys and car I imply by the word "unjust" that this is wrong, I am the person who has been wronged, and the specific wrong is a violation of my *right* to property. If you break a promise to help your classmate study for the examination, this is not only wrong, it is wrong because it is a violation of your classmate's *right* to your help, a right that you had conferred on him when you made the promise. If Edgar is treated better than Gertrude when their Physics professor gave a higher grade to Edgar than he gave to Gertrude even though they scored the same in all exams, he violated Gertrude's *right* to equal treatment.

5.5 The origin of the feeling of justice

Mill now returns to the question posed earlier (5.1). What is the origin of the feeling that accompanies the idea of justice? Is it a natural feeling, that is, is it part of our psychological makeup that we have these feelings when we witness an injustice? Could it have "grown up, by any known laws," out of the idea of justice itself? Or perhaps it "originated in considerations of general expediency"? (49).

Mill discards the last alternative, although he does not provide us with a reason. However, he is quick to add "though the sentiment does not, whatever is moral in it does." That is, although the feeling of injustice does not arise from considerations of general expediency (utility), whatever is moral in the feeling does so arise.

Thus, when we have a feeling of injustice, we believe that there is some definite person or persons who are the victims of the harm and we want to punish them.

Notice Mill's methodology here. He is not citing an empirical study to back up the above claim about feelings of injustice. He provides no data gleaned from observation and experience. Instead, he is making an analytical claim about the relationship of two ideas or concepts: "feelings of injustice" and "a desire to punish the person who one believes has caused harm to another." Mill's claim is that one could not have feelings of injustice unless she has a desire to punish the person who she believes has caused the harm.

Mill's second point is that the desire to punish a person who has caused harm to another is "a spontaneous outgrowth from two sentiments," both of which are natural or instinctive: the *impulse of self-defense* and *the feeling of sympathy* (50). There is an animal desire in all of us to "repel or retaliate" a hurt or damage to ourselves or to those with whom we sympathize, whether it be a family member, a friend, or one's village or tribe. In humans, this desire is widened "so as to include all persons". Humans have a "developed intelligence" which allows them to notice that "any conduct which threatens the security of the society generally is threatening to their own." This reaction calls forth our natural instinct of self-defense.

> *The same superiority of intelligence, joined to the power of sympathizing with human beings generally, enables him to attach himself to the collective idea of his tribe, his country, or mankind in such a manner that any act hurtful to them raise his instinct of sympathy and urges him to resistance* (50).

If we assume that these remarks are based on Mill's own observations, coupled with what contemporary scientists have learned about human social behavior, then there is ample evidence to support his claim that when one's country is threatened, many will rush to its defense. The huge increase in the number of Americans who flocked to military recruiting stations after the Japanese attack on Pearl Harbor (Hawaii) in 1941 is only one of many instances in human history of the social instinct to defend and retaliate.

Before summarizing the findings of this chapter, Mill wants to defend against the objection that when our sentiment (feeling) of justice is outraged, we think only of ourselves, not of "society at large or any collective interest." Mill's responds that although it is true that some feel resentment "merely because [they] feel pain," if resentment is really a moral feeling in which they are reacting to someone as blameworthy, they will feel that a universal moral rule has been violated, "a rule which is for the benefit of others as well as for their own" (51).

For example, I felt resentment when I learned a few years ago that a famous bicyclist had taken performance enhancing drugs to help him win several international biking competitions. When I say the words "I resent it," I am not reporting that I have a painful feeling called resentment. It would make no sense for me to say, "I resent only this athlete for cheating." What makes my feeling a *moral* feeling is that I imply a universal rule that no athlete should cheat in competition.

Mill concludes this section of the book with the following summary:

> *The idea of justice supposes two things: a rule of conduct and a sentiment which sanctions the rule. The first must be supposed common to all mankind and intended for their good. The other (the sentiment) is a desire that punishment may be suffered by those who infringe the rule. There is involved, in addition, the conception of some definite person who suffers by the infringement, whose rights (to use the expression appropriated to the case) are violated by it.*

There is a lot going on here. Suppose that Hortense has stolen Oscar's gold watch. When Percival accuses Hortense of injustice it must be *because* Hortense has violated a universal moral rule (in this case, theft), not a personal rule of Percival. Second, Percival's accusation is backed by a desire that Hortense be punished. Third, there must be some definite person (Oscar) or persons whose rights were violated by Hortense.

> *And the sentiment of justice appears to me to be the animal desire to repel or retaliate a hurt or damage to oneself or to those with whom one sympathizes, widened so as to include all persons, by the human capacity of intelligent self-interest. From the latter element the feeling derives its morality; from the former, its peculiar impressiveness and energy of self-assertion.* (51–52).

If Percival feels not only a personal desire to retaliate for Hortense's theft of Oscar's watch but also feels that *everyone* should "repel or retaliate" for hurts or damages *of this kind* to *any other person* in the same circumstances, then the feeling of retaliation becomes a *moral* feeling or sentiment, not a mere animal response.

5.6 The idea of a right

Mill had earlier said (5.5) that the obligation of justice is distinguished from moral obligation generally by its conceptual connection to the idea of a right. Once again: "Justice implies something which it is not only right to do, and wrong not to do, but what some individual person can claim as his right" (49).

This leaves us wondering about the nature of a right. What do we mean when we say that someone has a right to something, or that someone's right has been violated? Let's start with the latter phrase. Mill's analysis of what we mean by calling anything a violation of a person's right involves two elements: a hurt to some assignable person and a demand that the violator be punished. Thus, if we say that Sarah has violated Holden's right to property by stealing apples and oranges from his fruit trees, then we imply both that Holden has been hurt (harmed), and Sarah should be punished for this. Mill extracts from this scenario the following definition:

When we call anything a person's right, we mean that he has a valid claim on society to protect him in the possession of it, either by the force of law, or by that of education and opinion. If he has what we consider a sufficient claim, on whatever account, to have something guaranteed to him by society, we say that he has a right to it. (52)

The proof of this definition can be found in an example that Mill uses to show how we go about proving that either that someone does have a right or that they do not have the right that they say they have.

Thus, a person is said to have a right to what he can earn in fair professional competition, because society ought not to allow any other person to hinder him from endeavoring to earn in that manner as much as he can. But he has not a right to three hundred a year, though he may happen to be earning it; because society is not called on to provide that he shall earn that sum. On the contrary, if he owns ten thousand pounds three percent stock, he has a right to three hundred a year because society has come under an obligation to provide him with an income of that amount (52). [£300 in 1860 would be the equivalent of £35,000 in 2018].

Mill concludes this account by restating his definition: "To have a right, then, is, I conceive, to have something which society ought to defend me in the possession of." And to anyone who objects to this definition by asking "Why ought society do this?" Mill replies: "I can give no other answer than general utility." Thus, if someone wants to know why society ought to defend persons who endeavor to earn £300 or more in fair professional competition, Mill would answer that this promotes the greatest good for the greatest number. And if asked the same question about why society ought not to defend persons who want or demand to be given the same amount from the public coffers, Mill would answer that this would not promote the greatest good.

5.6.1 An imaginary conversation between Mill and Locke about natural rights

To illustrate the vast difference between Mill's account of the origin of rights and John Locke's theory of natural rights, consider the following imaginary conversation between these two great philosophers.

The scene: a pub in central London.

Locke: Good evening Mill. I just read *Utilitarianism* and was surprised and disappointed to find that you make no mention of *natural* rights. As you know, natural rights are a staple of liberal political philosophy and I wrote extensively about this in *Second Treatise of Government*.

Mill: And good evening to you Locke. How do you define a "natural" right?

L: A natural right is a right that a person has in the state of nature, as determined by the law of nature.

M: What is the state of nature? Is it a place where people live?

L: The words "state of nature" do not specify a place. They specify *a type of relationship* between two or more persons. It is a *pre-political relationship* in which there is no authorized third-party or umpire to whom people can turn to settle disputes about what laws exist or whether a law has been violated.

M: So, if there is a dispute about what rights are valid, there is no way to decide this?

L: Now I get to ask you a question. What do you mean by a *valid* right?

M: A valid right is a claim on society to protect the alleged right-holder from harm, by either the force of law or by education and opinion. For example, you and I *have* a right to life because a claim to have our life protected by the force of law is guaranteed by civil society. On the other hand, we *do not have* a right to be given a new horse and buggy every year because any such claim is not guaranteed by society.

L: I understand. So, based on what you just said, there are no valid rights in the state of nature. I agree that there is no mechanism for making a "claim on civil society," because by definition, there is no civil society. If anyone insists that what another person has done violates the law of nature, he is on his own. Most people in a state of nature are ignorant of the natural law anyway, and even if they think they know the law, there is no one they can call on for validation or for enforcement.

M: If there is no way to prove (validate) that something does or does not belong to a person "by right" in the state of nature, then your idea of a natural right seems to me to be so much empty noise. What would be the point of going around announcing that you have a right to life if you have no claim on others to protect you in the possession of it? As my godfather Jeremy Bentham once said, the idea of a natural right is "nonsense upon stilts."

L: That assessment is a bit harsh. The natural rights to life, liberty, health and possessions can still serve a purpose as an *ideal* set of rights that a society *ought* to adopt as positive law.

M: I agree that these rights ought to be legally enacted, but if you ask me why I agree, I can give no other reason than *general utility*.

L: Oh! I was going to say that they ought to be adopted because they are natural rights.

M: Isn't that what you said when we started this conversation?

5.7 The ambiguity of the internal oracle of justice

Non-utilitarians (like John Locke and Immanuel Kant) believe that justice is "totally independent of utility." Moreover, Mill writes, they believe that the dictates of justice "carry their evidence in themselves" and therefore, on questions of justice "there could be no controversy." Mill responds that if we adopt justice as our standard, then its application to any given case "would leave us in as little doubt as a mathematical demonstration" (54).

But there are many doubts. Mill gives several examples showing that there is as much difference of opinion, and as much doubt about what is just as there is about what is useful.

5.7.1 Amounts and kinds of punishment

Consider, for example, questions about the amount and manner of punishment. How much and what kind of punishment should legislators and judges apportion to criminal offenses? Some would reply that a *just* kind of punishment should be to do the same to the offender as the offender did to his victim. This is the retributive principle of "an eye for eye" and, applied to a conviction for murder, it demands that the only *just* punishment for this crime is to put the murderer to death.

It has been objected that this interpretation of the principle of justice could be used to justify an *unjust* sentence of death for someone who accidentally kills another. If the aim is to do the same to the offender as the offender did to the victim, then it is irrelevant that the offender killed the victim accidentally. He killed the victim, and that result can only be matched by taking the life of the killer: "a body for a body."

Second, it has been argued that the retributive principle of "an eye for an eye" is too narrow. There are many criminal offenses for which it has no meaningful application. Property crimes are at the top of the list. If a homeless person is convicted of arson for burning down a one-million-dollar house, there is nothing identical that the state can do to the arsonist that would match his crime (perhaps purchase a house, give the deed to the arsonist, and then burn down the house?).

On the other side of the argument about the application of pure justice to decide the appropriate manner and amount of punishment there are those who would have it proportioned to the moral guilt of the culprit. This assumes that there is a standard by which moral guilt can be measured, and on this point, there is extensive controversy. Consider the case of the man who draws a gun and fires point blank at his intended victim but fails to hit him. Some would argue that a failed attempt should be punished as severely as a successful murder, because in both cases there was an intent to kill. Others would use the principle of justice to argue that attempts to kill should be punished less severely because legal and moral guilt requires a dead body (*actus reus*) as well as a guilty mind (*mens rea*).

5.7.2 The abortion debate

Mill has several more examples in chapter V, each illustrating his point about the continuing controversy over the correct application of justice. I will leave these examples to the reader, and instead use an example of a contemporary controversy that was not contemplated by Mill or by other moral philosophers in the nineteenth century. I believe that it proves Mill's point that it is nearly impossible to get any unanimity about the morality of conduct by using justice alone to decide the case.

The example I have chosen is the long debate about the morality of abortion. The debate is as intense and as unsettled between those who use only the principle of justice and its corollaries as it is between them and those who use the principle utility and its corollaries. At one extreme are those who argue that the only relevant consideration is whether the abortion is the result of an intention to kill the fetus. The standard anti-abortion argument is this:

    1. Abortion is the intentional killing of an innocent human being.

    2. It is always wrong (unjust) to intentionally kill an innocent human being.

    3. The fetus from the moment of conception is an innocent human being.

    4. Therefore, it is always wrong (unjust) to kill the fetus.

    5. Therefore, abortion is always wrong (unjust).

But others who also use only the ideas of justice and rights in moral decision-making have challenged the standard argument. Some have objected to premise #1 by claiming that some abortions are not intended. Thus, if a pregnant woman has uterine cancer and the uterus must be removed, thereby killing the fetus inside, the intention of the physician is not to kill the fetus but to save the life of the woman. The death of the fetus is an expected but *unintended* consequence of the removal of the uterus.

Others have objected to premise #2, claiming that not all cases of killing an innocent human being are unjust. Suppose that the fetus is the unwanted product of a rape. We can all admit that this fetus is innocent, having nothing to do with occupying the rape victim's body. But it has been argued that it is entirely relevant to point out that the fetus has *no right* to occupy the rape victim's uterus. Its presence in her body is not woman's choice. She did not invite it in. Second, another important right that should be used in deciding this case is the *right to liberty*, the right of a woman to make the final choice about what happens in and to her own body, especially when a pregnancy is unwanted.

However, anti-abortionists respond that although the presence of the fetus in the woman's body is unwanted, the *right to life* should be broadly interpreted to include the right to be provided whatever the fetus requires to survive. They would also contend that the right to life trumps the right to liberty. Therefore, the right of the fetus to survive has priority over the right of a woman to make decisions about whether the fetus will remain in or be expelled from her body.

This controversy will not be decided in these pages. The point of using the preceding contemporary argument over the justice of abortion is to show that Mill is correct in saying that an application of justice alone is not simple, and certainly not at all like a mathematical demonstration. There is nothing in the idea of justice that will help us to prioritize the rights mentioned in a way that will settle the debate. It has certainly not settled the controversy between pro-life and pro-choice opponents over the morality of abortion.

5.8 Justice grounded on utility is the chief part of all morality

Appeals to the ideas of justice and rights alone are not sufficient to settle debates over abortion nor the debates mentioned by Mill in chapter V over amounts and kinds punishment (55), remuneration in cooperative industrial associations (56), and taxation policy (57). But, Mill argues, there is hope. These debates can be settled by a judicious use of the utility principle. Indeed, they must be settled in this way because justice is *not* an independent principle. Justice is firmly grounded in utility. The rules of justice are among the many corollaries of the principle of utility, although importantly distinct from other utility-based moral rules.

> *Justice is a name for certain classes of moral rules which concern the essentials of human well-being more nearly, and are therefore of more absolute obligation, than any other rules for the guidance of life; and the notion which we have found to be of the essence of the idea of justice—that of a right residing in an individual—implies and testifies to this more binding obligation.* (58)

The moral rules to which Mill refers include only those in which there is an individual right that implies and is reciprocal with the named obligation. At the top of the list are the class of rules "which forbid mankind to hurt one another, including wrongful interference with each other's freedom." These are the rules prohibiting murder, and several kinds of bodily harm, including assault, battery, harm to one's reputation (slander) and (these days) domestic violence. The moral rules prohibiting interference with each other's freedom include rape, kidnapping, enslavement, and paternalistic restrictions on adult behavior "for their own good." All of these rules imply an individual right not to be harmed in the manner specified, e.g. the right not to be harmed in one's life or in one's liberty.

Mill puts these rules at the top of the list of social utilities because "they are the main element in determining the whole of social feelings of mankind." If men and women did not observe these moral rules, then "everyone would see in everyone else an enemy against whom he must be perpetually guarding himself." Therefore, it is the rules prohibiting wrongful aggression or wrongful exercise of power over another which are *"the most marked cases of injustice, and those which give the tone to the feeling of repugnance which characterizes the sentiment."*

The next set of social utilities, somewhat lower on the scale, are those that involve obligations not to withhold from an individual something that is his due. This may be "a positive hurt, either in the form of direct suffering or of the privation of some good which he had reasonable ground, either of a physical or of a social kind, for counting upon" (59). Mill later mentions "a breach of friendship and a breach of promise" as examples. These examples are instances of the principle of "giving to each what they deserve, that is, good for good as well as evil for evil."

> *He who accepts benefits and denies a return of them when needed inflicts a real hurt by disappointing one of the most natural and reasonable of expectations, and one which he must at least tacitly have encouraged, otherwise the benefits would seldom have been conferred... Few hurts which human beings can sustain are greater, and none wound more, than when that on which they habitually and with full assurance relied fails them in the hour of need; and few wrongs are greater than this mere withholding of good..."* (59).

It follows from the duty to do to each what she deserves that "we should treat all equally well (when no higher duty forbids) who have deserved equally well of us, and that society should treat all equally well absolutely" (60). Mill writes that "this is the highest abstract standard of social and distributive justice," although he immediately reminds us that "this great duty has a deeper foundation" as a "direct emanation" from the greatest happiness principle.

> *It is involved in the very meaning of utility. That principle is a mere form of words without rational signification unless one person's happiness, supposed equal in degree (with the proper allowance made for kind) is counted for exactly as much as another's. These conditions being supplied, Bentham's dictum "everybody to count for one, nobody for more than one," might be written under the principle of utility as an explanatory commentary"* (60–61).

One criticism of this is that Mill is supplementing the utilitarian principle with an independent principle of distributive justice. If we are told that our obligation is to promote the greatest happiness for the greatest number, there is no implied instruction telling us to count each person's happiness exactly as much as another's. Mill has previously said that the happiness of Socrates counts for more than the happiness of a fool. (This is what he means when attaches the proviso "with the proper allowance made for kind.") But this seems to violate the principle "everybody counts for one, nobody more than one" because the preferences of those who have experienced both mental and physical pleasures count for more than those who have not (chapter II, 8–9). This poses a dilemma. Mill must either take back his thesis that the utilitarian principle implies an impartial distributive principle of justice or he must admit that it implies the non-utilitarian principle "some people count for more than one."

5.9 Cases that overrule a general maxim of justice

Mill is now satisfied that he has proved that justice is a name for a group of moral rules that "stand higher in the scale of social utility" than other rules, and therefore put a stronger obligation on us.

As noted several times above, these are the rules that are based on an individual's right. And yet there are some cases in which the demands of utility will overrule a general rule of justice.

> *Thus, to save a life, it may not only be allowable, but a duty, to steal or take by force the necessary food or medicine, or to kidnap and compel to officiate the only qualified medical practitioner (62).*

Let us assume that our utility calculations require that we steal food or medicine to save someone's life, or that we must kidnap at gunpoint the only doctor in town who refuses to leave his house at 3 a.m. to give necessary medical help to a dying child. Should we say that utility trumps justice in these cases, or should we say that justice aligns with utility in these cases, that is, it is "not unjust" to steal the food and medicine and "not unjust" to kidnap the doctor? Mill chooses the latter alternative, explaining that language allows this manner of describing what has happened because it allows us to avoid maintaining that there can be "laudable injustice" (62).

By presenting these examples Mill foresaw by more than 100 years a twentieth century thought experiment in ethics that is still under hot debate. It is called "The Trolley Problem," created in a 1967 essay by Philippa Foot. It has several versions. Here is one popular scenario:

Imagine an out-of-control trolley speeding down a steep hill. At the bottom of the hill five children are tied to the track. There is also a sidetrack that leads off the main track before the place where the five children are tied down. There is one child tied down on the sidetrack. You are standing far away from all of this, but you can see what is happening. You are gripping a lever that if pulled will immediately move the trolley onto the sidetrack.

Should you do nothing, or should you pull the lever? If you pull it, you will save the lives of five children, but the trolley will hit and kill the child on the sidetrack. If you do not pull it, the trolley will hit and kill the five children, and the child on the sidetrack will survive.

5.10 Questions for thought and discussion

1. If you feel outrage when hearing about or seeing an instance of injustice, how would you justify your feelings? What reasons would you give to convince others that they should share your feelings?

2. Why is the duty to give to charity "imperfect"? If it is imperfect, why do we have this duty at all?

3. Is the idea of a "natural right" nonsensical?

4. Do you agree with Mill that applications of the principle of justice are ambiguous, allowing of many different results? For example, some would say that it is clearly unjust that 40% of the wealth in the U.S. is owned by 1% of the population. Are they right about this or could an application of the justice principle give a different result?

5. Mill contends that justice is "grounded" in utility. How does he prove this? Do you find any flaws in his argument?

6. Mill does not want us to use the phrase "laudable injustice" to justify a decision to save a life by forcing the only qualified doctor to attend to the dying person. Instead, he wants us to say that the act of forcing was *not* unjust. But "not unjust" also means "does not violate any individual rights." Do you agree that no one's rights were violated when the doctor was kidnapped and compelled to attend to the dying child? (Assume that the child was not the doctor's patient and there are no civil laws requiring a medical doctor to come to the aid of people in distress).

7. In the trolley car scenario, assume that you have only two choices: either pull the lever or do not pull the lever. Which choice would involve violating an individual's right to life? Explain.

8. You are a software engineer at a leading automobile company. Your new task is to design software for a self-driving car. What software instructions would you recommend for "trolley problem" situations in which a choice must be made between killing one pedestrian to avoid swerving into a group of more than one, or vice versa?

References

Foot, Philippa. 1967. "The Problem of Abortion and the Doctrine of Double Effect." *Oxford Review* (Trinity), 5:5-15.

Bibliography for *Utilitarianism* and Utilitarian Theory

Crisp, Roger, 1997. *Mill on Utilitarianism.*, London: Routledge.

Darwall, Stephen, 1995. *Hume and the Invention of Utilitarianism*, University Park, PA: Penn State University Press.

Donner, Wendy, 1991. *The Liberal Self: John Stuart Mill's Moral and Political Philosophy*, Ithaca, NY: Cornell University Press.

– – –, 2011. "Morality, Virtue, and Aesthetics in Mill's Art of Life," in Ben Eggleston, Dale E. Miller, and David Weinstein (eds.) *John Stuart Mill and the Art of Life*, Oxford: Oxford University Press.

Driver, Julia, 2004. "Pleasure as the Standard of Virtue in Hume's Moral Philosophy." *Pacific Philosophical Quarterly.*, 85: 173–194.

– – –, 2011. *Consequentialism*, London: Routledge.

Gill, Michael, 2006. *The British Moralists on Human Nature and the Birth of Secular Ethics*, New York: Cambridge University Press.

Hruschka, Joachim, 1991. "The Greatest Happiness Principle and Other Early German Anticipations of Utilitarian Theory," *Utilitas*, 3: 165–77.

Long, Douglas, 1990. "'Utility' and the 'Utility Principle': Hume, Smith, Bentham, Mill," *Utilitas*, 2: 12–39.

Rosen, Frederick, 2003. "Reading Hume Backwards: Utility as the Foundation of Morals," in Frederick Rosen (ed.), *Classical Utilitarianism from Hume to Mill*, London: Routledge, 29–57.

Rosenblum, Nancy, 1978. *Bentham's Theory of the Modern State*, New York: Cambridge University Press.

Ryan, Alan, 1990. *The Philosophy of John Stuart Mill*, Amherst, NY: Prometheus Books.

Scarre, Geoffrey, 1996. *Utilitarianism*, London: Routledge.

Schneewind, J. B., 1977. *Sidgwick's Ethics and Victorian Moral Philosophy*, Oxford: Clarendon Press.

Schofield, Philip, 2006. *Utility and Democracy: the Political Thought of Jeremy Bentham*, Oxford: Oxford University Press.

Skorupski, John, 1989. *John Stuart Mill*, London: Routledge & Kegan Paul.

PART II *ON LIBERTY*

Chapter 6 Introductory (*On Liberty* I)

A man is convicted in a court of law for the crime of murder. He is sentenced to life in prison. Another man in ancient times named Socrates, is convicted for not believing in the official gods of the city-state in which he lives. He receives the penalty of death by poison. Four hundred years later, a man named Jesus of Nazareth is nailed to a cross and killed for the crime of heresy. Two thousand years after that, a young man in Montana is robbed, pistol-whipped and tortured by three other men when they learn that he is gay. A woman in England is shunned by the Muslim community in which she grew up for marrying a man who is of a different religion. A young woman in New York is verbally bullied on social media. She commits suicide.

The object of Mill's essay *On Liberty* is "Civil, or Social Liberty: the nature and limits of the power which can be legitimately exercised by society over the individual" (*On Liberty*, 1). The questions that Mill asks are questions of moral justification. What are the *justifiable* limits to the exercise of civil and social power over the individual? When *ought* society use civil and social power to intervene and when *ought it not* intervene? Or, from the perspective of the individual: What are the *justifiable* limits of individual liberty? How much liberty should an individual have in a civil society?

Society has two ways of exercising its power over the individual: *Civil Power* ("physical force in the form of legal penalties") and *Social Power* ("the moral coercion of public opinion"). The man who is given a life sentence for murder and the man who is executed for the crime of not believing in the official gods have both been subjected to civil power. The gay man who is tortured, the woman who is shunned and the young woman who is bullied are all the victims of social power (although in the case of the young gay man, the power used against him goes far beyond "moral coercion").

The questions posed by Mill are as important and relevant now as they were when Mill wrote *On Liberty*. In all countries it is justifiable to use physical force in the form of legal penalties for the crime of murder, but there are some countries that also believe it to be justifiable to use civil power against those who refuse to conform to the official state religion and to practices that are commanded by that religion. Although there are many countries in the Western world that pride themselves on their social toleration of gays, lesbians and others in the LGBTQ communities, there are still many instances in the West of intolerance of non-conforming attitudes, appearances and lifestyles. The intolerance is expressed not only in shunning (which often leads to depression and suicide), but sometimes in physical force. The rise of social media in the twenty-first century has also brought with it an alarming rise in hateful remarks, bullying and social shaming, fueled by anonymity.

6.1 Tyranny of the Majority

Mill observes that ancient concerns about individual liberty were mostly confined to efforts to protect against the tyranny of rulers who had either inherited their power or who had achieved it by conquest. The aim of those who resisted, Mill writes, "was to set limits to the power which the ruler should be suffered to exercise over the community; and this limitation was what they meant by liberty" (1-3). They accomplished this either by obtaining a recognition by the ruler of certain "political liberties or rights," or by requiring that important acts of the ruler be endorsed by her subjects or by representatives of her subjects.

> On June 1, 1215 the barons of England rebelled and pressured the king into signing the Magna Carta, a list of 63 clauses drawn up to limit John's power. "By declaring the sovereign to be subject to the rule of law and documenting the liberties held by "free men," the Magna Carta would provide the foundation for individual rights in Anglo-American jurisprudence." (D.M. Stenton)

The next step in the long effort to achieve individual liberty was to place political power in the hands of the people. As long as it was understood that the people were sovereign, they could either retain the power unto themselves ("direct democracy") or periodically delegate legislative and executive power to others ("representative democracy").

This was the time when, "in the progress of human affairs," men ceased to think it a necessity of nature that their governors should be an independent power opposed in interest to themselves (2). The governors or rulers were now identified with the people, and the interest and will of the rulers was no longer opposed to but identical with the will and interests of the people.

This identity of will and interests led to the idea that there was no longer the threat of tyranny. How, it was asked, could the nation tyrannize over itself? Where there is self-government (it was said) "the people have no need to limit their power over themselves" (3).

This notion, Mill claims, is dangerously false. It completely fails to recognize the insidious phenomenon of "the tyranny of the majority."

> *The 'people' who exercise the power are not always the same people with those over whom it is exercised, and the 'self-government' spoken of is not the government of each by himself but of each by all the rest. The will of the people, moreover, practically means the will of the most numerous or the most active part of the people--the majority, or those who succeed in making themselves accepted as the majority; ...and in political speculations 'the tyranny of the majority' is now generally included among the evils against which society requires to be on guard (4).*

There are different kinds of majorities and different ways they can suppress and dominate a minority. There are the obvious cases in which a majority of citizens in a democracy have created legislation to restrict the liberty of a minority (for example, segregation laws enacted in most southern states after the Civil War, restricting the freedom of adult African-Americans to vote and the freedom of their children to attend school with white children). There are less obvious cases in which there is a tyranny not of law, but of "prevailing opinion and feeling." Mill writes that the latter form of tyranny is "more formidable than many kinds of political oppression" (4).

> ...since, though not usually upheld by such extreme penalties, it leaves fewer means of escape, penetrating much more deeply into the details of life, and enslaving the soul itself....the tendency of society to impose, by other means than civil penalties, its own ideas and practices as rules of conduct on those who dissent from then, to fetter the development, and, if possible prevent the formation, of any individuality not in harmony with its ways, and compel all characters to fashion themselves upon the model of its own (4-5).

One example of the tyranny of the "prevailing opinion and feeling" is religious intolerance. The victims are usually atheists.

> Nearly a majority of Americans would, if they had their way, deny freedom of speech to those who are against all religions and churches. For many Americans, atheism is an illegitimate political position and must therefore be prohibited from entering the marketplace of ideas (Gibson, 2009).

After the September 11, 2001 attacks on the Twin Towers in New York, there have been many reports of rising amounts of intolerance toward Muslims and people who "look like" a Muslim.

> We have reached the point where a head scarf, a full beard or even a family name engenders so much animosity – an animosity that is leading to hate crimes and anti-religious and ethnic violence. Most troubling is that the volume and frequency of these incidents seems to be increasing (Zaffar, 2016)

Non-conformity is defined as "deviating in (appearance and/or behavior) and/or lifestyle relative to a group of humans with normative standards." The key phrase here is "relative to a group." Ultimately, nonconformity is relative to the norms of a group and if your group is small enough then you may be conforming to the norms of the small group but not conforming to the norms of a larger group or society in general. (S. Bapir-Tardy, 2016).

The atmosphere became even more toxic in the United States after the 2016 general election. There was a significant rise in the number of hate groups (defined as groups that "have beliefs or practices that attack or malign an entire class of people, typically for their immutable characteristics" Southern Poverty Law Center). Some of these groups emerged from anonymity, probably because they sense that their views are now shared or at least tolerated by a wider audience. The August 12, 2017 march in Charlottesville, Virginia, sponsored by white supremacists, and the resulting violent clashes, is only one of hundreds of examples of contemporary racist intolerance and discrimination. (CBS News).

There are many examples of ways that majorities will use negative attitudes of disapproval and hate to force conformity to social norms. Examples include: shunning, scorning, evading, shaming, censuring, reprehending, rebuking and condemning.

6.2 The harm-to-others principle

If it is agreed that there ought to be protection against "the prevailing opinion and feeling," the question is where to place the limit to "the legitimate interference of collective opinion with individual independence" (5).

To this question, Mill gives an answer in the form of "one very simple principle," stipulating the conditions under which society is justified in interfering with individual liberty:

> [T]he sole end for which mankind are warranted, individually or collectively, in interfering with the liberty of action of any of their number, is self-protection... [T]he only purpose for which power can be rightfully exercised over any member of a civilized community, against his will, is to prevent harm to others... The only part of the conduct of anyone, for which he is amenable to society, is that which concerns others (9).

Mill does not give a name to this principle, but later commentators are nearly unanimous in calling it either the Harm Principle or, more accurately, the Harm-to-Others Principle [HOP].

6.3 Other liberty-limiting principles

When Mill writes that harm to others is "the sole end" for which a society can use compulsion and control over the individual he means to *exclude* other ends that have been or might be used to justify this control. Here are a few of several actual and possible principles (Feinberg, 33; Houlgate, 107; Altman, 159).

6.3.1 Harm-to-self

The first and most prominent principle that refers to alternative ends is known as the Harm-to-Self Principle [HSP].

HSP does not deny that harm to others is *one* justification for limiting liberty. But it does deny that it is the *only* justification. Thus, a defender of HSP might make the following addition to the short list of liberty-limiting principles:

> A second purpose for which power can be rightfully exercised over any member of a civilized community, against his will, is to prevent him from doing harm to himself (HSP)

The use of *legal* power to either prevent someone from doing harm to herself is what is known as *legal paternalism* (LP). The word "paternalism" has its origin in parent-child relationships in which the parent has the moral and legal authority to prevent their child from doing harm to herself. LP is used as a justification for laws requiring adult motorcyclists and their passengers to use certified headgear, and laws requiring motorists and their passengers to wear seatbelts. Paternalistic laws are also enacted to prohibit the use of certain mind-altering drugs, for example, marijuana (but not wine or spirits).

> BASE jumping is parachuting or wingsuit flying from a fixed structure or cliff. It is one of the most dangerous of all life-risking sports. In 2016, 31 jumpers died, a fatality rate that spurred practitioners to dub the 2016 summer as "Wingsuit BASE Killing Season." (Bisharat, 2016). Should we try to stop this by making BASE jumping illegal, or publicly shaming those we attempt it? If we accept Mill's suggestion that there is no justification for limiting an individual's liberty "for his own good," then the most we can do is to reason with the jumpers, persuade or even beg them not to take such risks. Mill contends that compulsion, in any form, either by law or opinion, is always morally unjustifiable as a response to conduct which is not harmful to others.

But Mill soundly rejects HSP in all of its forms (including LP). Although it is justifiable to exercise legal or social power over a member of a civilized community to prevent harm to others,

> *...His own good, either physical or moral, is not a sufficient warrant. He cannot rightfully be compelled to do or forbear because it will be better for him to do so, because it will make him happier, because in the opinions of others, to do so would be wise, or even right. These are good reasons for remonstrating with him, or reasoning with him or persuading him, or entreating him, but not for compelling him, or visiting him with any evil in case he do otherwise. To justify that, the conduct from which it is desired to deter him must be calculated to produce evil to someone else. The only part of conduct of anyone for which he is amenable to society is that which concerns others. In the part which*

concerns only himself, his independence is, of right, absolute. Over himself, over his own body and mind, the individual is sovereign. (9)

6.3.2 *Legal or social moralism*

The second principle that is part of legal and moral fabric of many countries has as its object to prevent and punishes immoral but not harmful conduct. It is commonly known as Legal Moralism [LM]. In addition to conduct that causes harm to others, LM proposes other actions which are immoral but do not cause harm to others. This category of human behavior includes consensual conduct between adults in which there is no victim, for example fornication, adultery, homosexual behavior (sodomy), prostitution, and polygamy.

> In August of 2004, John R. Bushey Jr. was finally brought to justice in a small courthouse in Luray, Va. Bushey, the former town attorney, stood before the court as an accused criminal with reporters from all over the state in attendance. The charge was adultery. Like 23 other states, Virginia still might prosecute if a husband or wife has consensual sex outside the marriage. Ten states, including Virginia, have anti-fornication statutes as well, prohibiting sex before marriage. Like many fundamentalist Islamic states, the United States uses criminal penalties to police the morality of its citizens (Turley).

Mill's response to this is in the first sentence of the quote at 6.3.1: "His own good, either physical *or moral*, is not a sufficient warrant." Neither the law nor society have any justification for legal or social intervention because they are of the opinion that the conduct with which they interfere is believed by them to be morally wrong. The most that society can do is to attempt to persuade the fornicators and adulterers not to have sex outside of marriage or not to be unfaithful to their spouse, but not to use legal sanctions or social pressure to behave otherwise.

6.3.3 *The offense principle*

The third category of actions that are frequently prohibited by law or social opinion is conduct that is offensive to others. Some of acts thought to be offensive are victimless consensual sex, and thus would include the immoral conduct previously discussed. The only difference is that the emphasis is put on the *feeling of being offended* by the conduct, not necessarily the belief that the conduct is immoral. Other examples of conduct alleged to be offensive are public nudity, public sexual behavior, public excretion, desecration of the flag, obscene language and pornographic displays.

The test of adopting offensiveness as a liberty-limiting principle is whether Mill would consider "being offended" as a way of being harmed. Does reading or viewing pornographic material cause harm to viewer? If "a rich homosexual uses a billboard on Times Square to promulgate to the general populace the techniques and pleasure of sodomy," would this display cause harm to those who find it offensive? (Feinberg, 43, quoting Schwartz). If a protester at a rally burns the American flag as a symbolic means of expressing his opinion, should he be punished?

Gregory Lee Johnson burned an American flag outside of the convention center where the 1984 Republican National Convention was being held in Dallas, Texas. Johnson burned the flag to protest the policies of President Ronald Reagan. He was arrested and charged with violating a Texas statute that prevented the desecration of a venerated object, including the American flag, if such action were likely to incite anger in others. A Texas court tried and convicted Johnson. He appealed, arguing that his actions were "symbolic speech" protected by the First Amendment. The Supreme Court agreed to hear his case and ruled in his favor. The 5–4 court majority noted that freedom of speech protects actions that society may find very offensive, but society's outrage alone is not justification for suppressing free speech (Texas v Johnson).

6.4 Children, the mentally handicapped, and backward societies

Mill adds the proviso that this doctrine "is meant only to apply to human beings in the maturity of their faculties." It does not apply to children or other persons "who are still in a state to require being taken care of by others."

Mill also writes that he will "leave out of consideration those backward states of society in which the race itself may be considered as in its nonage," implying that there are such "backward states" or "races."

Mill was a key inheritor of the liberal justification of Empire. Like his father, he was a career employee of the East India Company. In this vein, Mill goes on to declare in the same paragraph, "despotism is a legitimate mode of government in dealing with barbarians, provided the end be their improvement, and the means justified by actually effecting that end. Liberty, as a principle, has no application to any state of things anterior to the time when mankind has become capable of being improved by free and equal discussion."

The last sentence of the above quote explains why Mill would void all legislation based on HSP. It is because those *with the capacity* to be mentally and morally improved by free and equal discussion should not be interfered with by legal or social restrictions.

6.5 Utility as the ultimate justification of the harm principle

It should come as no surprise that Mill would use "harm to others" as a justification for civil and social intervention in human conduct. The rule that tells us not to harm others is among those moral rules that collectively are "higher in the scale of social utility and are therefore of more paramount obligations, than any others" (*Utilitarianism*, ch. V, 62). In fact, the rule is so high in the scale of social utility that we commonly use the words "*unjust*" and "violation of *a right*" to evaluate an incident in which one person does harm to others.

Although the obligation not to harm others is high in the scale of social utility, conflicts still exist which can only be finally resolved by an appeal to the utilitarian principle (to promote the greatest balance of pleasure over pain). This is because there is more than one way to harm others. There is not only a rule or obligation not to harm another *in their life*, but also a rule or obligation not to harm another *in their liberty*.

> The moral rules which forbid mankind to hurt one another (in which we must never forget to include a wrongful interference with each other's freedom) are more vital to human well-being than any other maxims... (*Utilitarianism*, 58).

These two rules may come into conflict, for example, when civil society restricts the liberty of individuals by punishing and threatening to punish those who attempt to assault or kill others. When we calculate the pain of those who are harmed by the conduct of others and we balance it against the pain suffered by those whose desire to do harm is legally thwarted, Mill assumes that the calculation will always come out in favor of those who are harmed. We have a right to liberty and a right to life, but one is not justified by using one's liberty to take a life, unless in self-defense.

6.6 Harm to self is not a justification for intervention

While placing prohibitions on harm that are "high in the scale of social utility," Mill finds only *disutility* in legal and social attempts to interfere with individual liberty for a person's "own good."

In defense of this absolute prohibition, Mill begins by giving a brief outline of the kind of conduct that he insists must be protected from intervention. He divides them into three spheres:

1. *Liberty of conscience*, comprising "*liberty of thought and feeling, absolute freedom of opinion and sentiment on all subjects, practical or speculative, scientific, moral or theological, and the liberty of expressing and publishing opinions...*" (11).

2. *Liberty of tastes and pursuits*, comprising "*framing the plan of our life to suit our own character, of doing what we like...so long as what we do does not harm [others]."* (12)

3. *Liberty of combination* among individuals, comprising "*freedom to unite for any purpose not involving harm to others; the persons combining being supposed to be of full age and not forced or deceived."* (12)

Mill says of all three spheres of liberty that:

> No society in which these liberties are not, on the whole, respected is free, whatever may be its form of government; and none is completely free in which they do not exist absolute and unqualified. (12)

Thus, a society that regards itself as "completely free" must not only allow people to combine for the purpose of stamp collecting, but also for the purpose of publishing and disseminating anti-Semitic literature. It must not only allow people to pursue their interest in birds and combine with others into bird watching clubs, but society must also not interfere with those who want to put on the hood and robe of the Ku Klux Klan and march in public chanting the language of hate.

The disutility of prohibitions on any of the three liberties enumerated above is encapsulated in this single sentence:

> Mankind are greater gainers by suffering each other to live as seems good to themselves than by compelling each to live as seems good to the rest. (12)

What does mankind gain in both cases and *how* is the gain for the former greater than the gain in the other? The answer to these questions is not achieved by doing a simple utility calculation, nor does Mill tell us the how to do the calculation. However, it is important to recall from *Utilitarianism*, that happiness is not to be identified with "a continuity of highly pleasurable excitement." (Mill, *Util.*, 12). Instead, Mill defines a happy life as

> ...an existence made up of few and transitory pains, many and various pleasures, with a decided predominance of the active over the passive, and having as the foundation of the whole, not to expect more from life than it is capable of bestowing (Mill, *Util.*, 13)

This still does not lead to the conclusion that "suffering each other to live as seems good to themselves" produces a greater balance of pleasure over pain than the balance produced by "compelling each to live as seems good to all the rest." It is not inconceivable that the balance in each case could be the same, or that the balance could be on the side of the compelled group. Since Mill produces no evidence to prove what appears to be an empirical claim, we must refrain from judgement.

Perhaps the best way to rescue Mill is to recall his claim that "some kinds of pleasure are more desirable and more valuable than others." The standard that Mill uses to place mental pleasures as superior to physical pleasures is that of "competent acquaintance." It is an application of this standard that the "manner of existence which employs the higher faculties" is preferable to a manner of existence that employs the lower faculties, and thus is more desirable than the former -- because those who have had experience of both kinds of life prefer it.

> *Better to be a Socrates dissatisfied than a fool satisfied...And if the fool...is of a different opinion, it is because [he] knows [his] own side of the question. The other party knows both sides.* (Mill, *Util.*, 10)

From what we know about Socrates from the dialogues of Plato, it seems safe to assume that having had experience of both systems, Socrates and others who have had the same experiences would vote to reject a paternalistic system that compels each person to live as seems good to the majority. It is this that Mill means when he writes that he is appealing to utility "in the largest sense, grounded on the permanent interests of man as a progressive being." A utility calculation that counts only the votes of those who live and prefer a manner of existence employing the higher faculties will want to nurture, not stifle the promise of satisfying these interests. They will want liberty to flourish. This can only be accomplished in a system that gives individuals absolute freedom to pursue the liberties of conscience, tastes and pursuits, and freedom of combination.

[Mill has more to say about this, as it relates to human development and self-realization in chapters 7 (II) and 8 (III).]

6.7 Causing and failing to prevent harm to others

Society may not only rightfully compel persons to refrain from doing harm, but it may also rightfully compel "positive acts for the benefit of others" (10). Examples of the latter include giving evidence in court, bearing one's fair share in the defense of the country, and performing "certain acts of individual beneficence, such as saving a fellow creature's life or interposing to protect the defenseless against ill-usage" (10).

If we are to fit this into HOP, then "doing harm to others" implies not only *causing harm* to others by an act of commission (for example, assault, murder, theft), but it also implies *preventing harm* to others. We are required to give evidence in court because not giving evidence would be harmful to the judicial goal of achieving a just outcome of the case. We are required to bear our fair share in defense of the country because not to do so would put an unjust burden on those who do their fair share and on the protection of the country itself. We have a duty to save a fellow creature's life because if we have no such duty they may suffer the ultimate harm – death.

Mill is aware of the objection that refraining from saving someone's life is not the moral equivalent of killing someone. If a small child is drowning in a pool and a passerby decides not to save her, even though he could do this without causing harm to himself, it is still true that if she dies, *he* did not kill her.

This objection ignores the fact that Mill is a utilitarian. The descriptions of what happened as "killed her" or "did not save her" are irrelevant. All that matters is that *death* is the consequence of a failure to save the child. It is the same consequence (death) that would have resulted if the passerby had actively drowned the child. It should come as no surprise that the utility calculation that demands that we ought to refrain from killing others is identical to the utility calculation that demands that we ought to save or attempt to save others when we can accomplish this without doing harm to ourselves (we must avoid situations in which the attempt to exercise control produces "other evils, greater than those which it would prevent").

> Minnesota and Vermont are the only states in the U.S.A. that have "good Samaritan" laws requiring citizens to help those in need. Other states give immunity from liability to medical professionals who give treatment in emergency situations, and to private citizens who call for emergency care and administer rescue drugs to persons who have overdosed opioids. (National Conference of State Legislatures, 2017)

When we combine Mill's acceptance of an obligation to perform "certain acts of individual beneficence" with his earlier rejection of the harm-to-self principle, both endorsed on utilitarian grounds, we may wonder why it would not be beneficent to regulate or prohibit activities that might cause serious harm or death, for example, requiring a doctor's prescription as a condition for obtaining certain drugs for one's own use, prohibiting persons from climbing the steep face of a mountain cliff without climbing gear, or closing beaches to all swimmers when sharks are sighted? If utility is our guide, why don't these interventions in individual liberty promote a greater balance of happiness over unhappiness than non-intervention?

6.8 The sphere of actions affecting only oneself

An objection to the harm-to-others principle is that all or almost all of everything a person does affects others in some way. The man who dies of an overdose of opioids might have harmed only himself – until we learn that he leaves behind two small children who were in his care. The woman who dies in an automobile accident because she failed to wear a seatbelt might, for the same reason, have harmed not only herself, but young children who depended on her as well.

How, then, are we to draw a distinction between doing harm to oneself and harm to others? Is there a bright line between these harms that can guide a legislator? Mill admits *"whatever affects himself may affect others through himself"* but promises that this objection will "receive consideration" in a future chapter (11).

6.9 Questions for thought and discussion

1. Mill says that the tyranny of the majority in a democracy is as repressive as the tyranny of dictatorships. Why does he say this? Do you agree? Do democratic governments have any ways to prevent majorities from tyrannizing minorities that dictatorial regimes do not have?

2. Mill writes that the tyranny of social "opinions and feelings" does as much or even more damage to individual liberty than the tyranny of repressive laws. What are some examples of social tyranny? How has the rise of social media fueled this tyranny? Is there any way you can think of that social tyranny can be stopped?

3. Why would utilitarians endorse HOP and reject HSP? If you are acquainted with other ethical theories (for example, John Locke's natural law theory), do you think they would arrive at the same conclusion?

4. Is it logically possible to expand the harm-to-others principle to require conduct that benefits others (e.g. rescuing a drowning child), while at the same time rejecting the harm-to-self principle?

5. Is there a plausible distinction you can make between acts that harm others and acts that harm only oneself? Explain.

6. The first amendment to the U.S. Constitution says, "Congress shall make no law respecting an establishment of religion; or prohibiting the free exercise thereof; or abridging the freedom of speech, or of the press; or the right of the people peaceably to assemble, and to petition the Government for a redress of grievances." Is this consistent with HOP?

References

Bapir-Tardy, Savin. 2016. The practice of shunning and its consequences. *Sedaa-Our Voices.* http://www.sedaa.org/2016/11/the-practice-of-shunning-and-its-consequences/

Bisharat, Andrew. 2016. Why are so many base jumpers dying? *National Geographic.* August 30, 2016. https://www.nationalgeographic.com/adventure/features/why-are-so-many-base-jumpers-dying/

CBS News. 2018. White supremacist rallies lead to violence. https://www.cbsnews.com/pictures/white-supremacist-rallies-in-charlottesville-virginia/

Feinberg, Joel. 1973. *Social Philosophy.* Englewood Cliffs, New Jersey: Prentice-Hall.

Goldston, Linda. 2006 and 2016. Berkeley 'naked guy' had a charismatic life and a tragic death. *East Bay Times.* https://www.eastbaytimes.com/2006/11/15/berkeley-naked-guy-had-charismatic-life-and-a-tragic-death-2/

National Conference of State Legislatures, 2017. Drug overdose immunity and good samaritan laws. http://www.ncsl.org/research/civil-and-criminal-justice/drug-overdose-immunity-good-samaritan-laws.aspx

Southern Poverty Law Center. 2016. Hate groups: state totals. https://www.splcenter.org/hate-map

Stenton, Doris Mary. 2018. Magna Carta: history, summary and importance. *Encyclopedia Brittanica.* https://www.britannica.com/topic/Magna-Carta

Texas v Johnson 1984. 491 U.S. 397.

Turley, Jonathan. 2004. Of lust and the law. *Washington Post.*

Chapter 7 Liberty of Thought and Discussion (*On Liberty* II)

Censorship is defined as "the suppression or prohibition of any parts of books, films, news, etc. that are considered obscene, politically unacceptable, or a threat to security" (Oxford). The definition does not include all of the things or events that are suppressed, for example, lectures and live theater performances; nor does it cover all of the reasons that have been given for suppression, for example, that the speech is considered offensive, that it is hate speech or that it might incite people to riot.

Censorship throughout history:

- In ancient societies in both the West (Greece) and East (China), censorship was considered a "legitimate instrument for regulating the moral and political life of the population" (Newth, 2010).
- Free speech was considered to be a distinct heretical threat to the Christian church, especially after the invention of the printing press in the mid-15th century.
- The creation of the postal service in 1464 significantly aided the dissemination of ideas, but for this reason it was used by authorities as an instrument for ideas that required censorship.
- Newspapers have been censored in many countries almost from the time that the first newspaper was published in 1610 in Switzerland. (One particularly brutal method of suppressing news has been to murder the editors, journalists and media workers who report it.)
- Books and the libraries that house them have long been targets of censorship from ancient times. The method of censorship in several cases was to burn the books or set fire to the entire library. "The entire collection of the University of Oxford library in 1683 was burned on direct orders from the king" and nearly 250 years later in Nazi Germany, "any book written by a Jewish author, communist or humanist, was fed to the flames." (Newth, 2010).

7.1 Contemporary examples of free speech controversies

Libraries and books are no longer burned in the West, and news reporting and editorial opinions in newspapers and on the radio, television and the internet are relatively free from government intervention. But there are still many on-going controversies over justifiable restrictions on freedom of expression. Here are six examples.

- In California, the state legislature is attempting to force so-called crisis pregnancy centers, which exist primarily to dissuade women from having abortions, to display prominent advertisements detailing the availability of state-funded abortions. "The centers say the law violates their right to free speech by forcing them to convey messages at odds with their beliefs. The law's defenders say the notices combat incomplete or misleading information provided by the clinics." (Liptak, 2017).

- Free speech on campus is under attack from both the right and the left of the political spectrum. In 2017, Kenneth Storey was fired from the University of Tampa after tweeting that Hurricane Harvey was "instant karma" for Texans who voted Republican. Tampa citizens complained about this to the university president, who promptly fired Professor Storey. (Weiner, 2017).

- The European Union has adopted what is generally referred to as the "right to be forgotten," based on a 2014 ruling of the European Court of Justice. At the heart of that ruling is the determination that Google and other search engines must remove links to content published years before that was harmful to personal reputation but that is now deemed to be "irrelevant or no longer relevant." It has been objected that the word "true" has been replaced by the word "irrelevant," thereby undermining the freedom of the press (including search engines) to widely disseminate and the people to discover information about past events. Because the published material was true, "viewed through American eyes, every aspect of the court's ruling would have been at odds with the First Amendment" (Abrams, 2018).

- In the United Kingdom hate speech is widely criminalized. Communications that are abusive, threatening, or insulting, or which target someone based on his race, religion, sexual orientation, or other attribute, are forbidden. Penalties for hate speech in the U.K. include fines and imprisonment. (Legal Dictionary)

- In Germany, *Volksverhetzung* ("incitement of the people") is a concept in German criminal law that bans incitement to hatred against segments of the population. It often applies to (though not limited to) trials relating to Holocaust denial in Germany. In addition, *Strafgesetzbuch* 86a outlaws various symbols of "unconstitutional organizations", such as Nazi symbolism or the ISIS flag.

- And last but not least, the rap superstar Kanye West was recently condemned by many of his fans for saying "400 years of slavery sounds like a choice" (Amatulli, 2018).

7.2 A thought experiment

Mill begins his inquiry with a thought experiment. He asks his readers to imagine a government that announces to the citizens that it will never silence any expression of opinion unless the people want it silenced. Mill's question is whether this transfer of the power to suppress an opinion from the government to the people makes any future suppression legitimate.

Mill's answer is that "the power itself is illegitimate." It does not matter in the least that the government is entirely at one with the people.

> *If all mankind minus one were of one opinion, mankind would be no more justified in silencing that one person than he, if he had the power, would be justified in silencing mankind.* (16)

Society would be no more justified in silencing the holocaust denier than the denier, if he had the power, would be justified in silencing all of society.

7.3 The definition of "differences of opinion"

When Mill uses the phrase "differences of opinion" he is talking about subjects "on which difference of opinion is *possible*" (35). Where there are genuine differences of opinion, "the truth depends on a balance to be struck between two sets of conflicting reasons." Thus, the statements "All triangles have three sides," "2 + 3 = 5," and "All bachelors are unmarried males" are *not* opinions because there are no conflicting reasons one could give for saying that they are not true. They are true *a priori*, "requiring nothing to command assent except that the meaning of the terms be understood" (Mill, *Util.*, 3). If you understand the terms "bachelor," and "unmarried," that is all you need to confirm the truth of the statement "All bachelors are unmarried males." There are no reasons one could give for saying that "Some bachelors are married," because this statement expresses a contradiction in terms.

This leaves an enormous number of subjects on which difference of opinion is possible, beginning with disputes in *natural philosophy*, or what we now call the physical sciences, for example, physics, astronomy, biology.

> "The term 'natural philosophy', which is a rendering of Aristotle's 'physics', was appropriated in the 17th century to the new natural science of Galileo and Newton... Apparently this usage continued in England when it had become obsolete in other countries. And even now there are survivals of this usage....and there are professors of 'natural philosophy' who are engaged in nuclear research." (Encyclopaedia Britannica, 1966)

Mill writes that in natural philosophy, "there is always some other explanation possible of the same facts" (35). Contemporary scientists understand that their explanations are "theories" or "hypotheses," that can and should be confirmed and tested by experimentation and careful observation. It is generally understood that there is no "absolute truth" in the physical sciences.

If there is no absolute truth in the physical sciences, then why do so many pretend that they know the absolute truth in "morals, religion, politics, social relations and the business of life," subjects that are "infinitely more complicated"? These are certainly the subjects to which the word "opinion" nicely attaches itself. If we are prepared to preface our statements about a subject that falls within one of these categories with the words "I am of the opinion that," we are signaling to our interlocutors that we will suspend judgment until we hear the counter-arguments. Unfortunately, this is not the common practice, especially in religion and politics.

> *Three-fourths of the arguments for every disputed opinion consist in dispelling the appearances which favor some opinion different from it...He who knows only his own side of the case knows little of that. His reasons may be good, and no one may have been able to refute them. But if he is equally unable to refute the reasons on the opposite side, if he does not so much as know what they are, he has no ground for preferring either opinion (35).*

7.4 Reasons why no opinion should be silenced

Mill sums up his entire argument for freedom of opinion and freedom of expression of opinion thus:

> [T]he peculiar evil of silencing the expression of an opinion is that it is robbing the human race. ...If the opinion is right, they are deprived of the opportunity of exchanging error for truth; if wrong, they lose, what is almost as great a benefit, the clearer perception and livelier impression of truth produced by its collision with error (16).

Much later in chapter II (50), Mill links freedom of opinion and freedom of expression of opinion to "the mental well-being of mankind" as its *necessary condition*, for the reasons cited below, the first two of which repeat the reasons given in the previous quote. In reviewing these reasons, we must do so in the context of Mill's "one very simple principle": harm-to-others (6.2). Are there opinions that, if expressed, are so dangerous that they can cause harm to others? Are there any opinions that, if thought about, might be so dangerous to the thinker that society must take steps to prevent her from being exposed to these opinions?

A. First, the opinion that is silenced might be true. "To deny this is to assume our own infallibility." No one is infallible, and no opinion should be silenced, no matter how certain a majority of the people are about its falsehood.

B. Second, if the silenced opinion is false, "it may contain a portion of the truth." By the very act of silencing it, we lose the opportunity of discussion and "the collision of adverse opinions" that could and often does, expose the remainder of the truth.

    C. Third, even if the received opinion be not only true, but the whole truth, if contrary opinions are prohibited, then we eventually forget the rational basis for the opinion, and it will revert to "the manner of prejudice."

    D. Fourth, as an extension of the third reason, "the meaning of the doctrine itself will be in danger of being lost or enfeebled and deprived of its vital effect on the character and conduct." The opinion will become dogma, thereby preventing "the growth of any real and heart-felt conviction from reason of personal experience."

Using (A) as an example, we can use "mental well-being" as a premise in an argument for the conclusion that there is no justification for silencing an opinion:

1. A silenced opinion believed to be false might be true.
2. If a silenced opinion that might be true *is true*, then people lose the opportunity of exchanging error for truth.
3. If people lose the opportunity of exchanging error for truth, this denies them an opportunity to improve their mental well-being.
4. There is no justification for denying people an opportunity to improve their own mental well-being.
5. Therefore, there is no justification for silencing an opinion believed to be false.

Premise #4 is an application of the harm-to-others principle and the implied claim that *in the part of one's conduct which concerns only oneself,* one's independence is, of right, absolute. Absent a showing that denying people an opportunity to improve their own well-being prevents harm to others, there is no justification for silencing opinions believed to be false. If a person does not want to seize the chance to improve her mental well-being, that is her decision to make, not ours.

    Another way of looking at Mill's argument is to interpret the silencing of an opinion as a kind of compulsion. When I am kept ignorant of an opinion I am thereby compelled to remain in ("trapped in") my own world of opinions. I am not given the opportunity of breaking out of that world to visit and examine alternative opinions. To repeat a point already made, if there is no evidence that keeping people ignorant of alternative opinions prevents them from doing harm to others, then the only justifications that remain are paternalistic; for example, it is "better" for me not to see alternative opinions, it will "make me happier," because in the opinions of others, trapping me in my own world of opinions "would be wise or even right" (9).

    Imagine a young man who believes in God in an isolated community in which everyone believes in God. He has never heard any arguments for believing in God,

nor does he say that he believes in God "because everyone else believes in God."
He just believes what he has been taught (Plantinga,33).

Each of the other three reasons (B), (C) and (D) for not silencing opinions contain
arguments with a similar structure. Each depends on the principle that it is always
wrong to prevent a person from achieving mental well-being or self-improvement.
And all lead to the same conclusion that silencing opinions, whether they are true,
false, or "the whole truth," is always unjustifiable.

The second of the four reasons (B), for example, can be structured like this:

1. A silenced opinion that is false might yet contain "a portion of the truth."
2. A portion of truth contained in an opinion can only be discovered by its
   collision with adverse opinions.
3. Silencing a false opinion keeps people ignorant of adverse opinions.
4. Keeping people ignorant of adverse opinions denies them the opportunity to
   discover that portion of the truth contained in the false opinion.
5. Knowledge of even a portion of the truth is always conducive to an
   improvement of one's mental well-being
6. There is no justification for denying people an opportunity to improve their
   own mental well-being.
7. Therefore, there is no justification for silencing an opinion that is false.

There is much more in (A) – (D) to discuss. We might wonder how a false opinion
has a "portion of the truth" and how a "collision" with alternative opinions releases
that portion. Mill gives examples drawn from clashes in religion between
traditionalists and heretics and examples from politics drawn from clashes between
conservatives and progressives. My example is drawn from a single contemporary
opinion that has met a great deal of resistance. As noted in section 2.1, the rap star
Kanye West made a recent claim that "400 years of slavery sounds like a choice." It
was immediately challenged and loudly deplored by many who wrote that West
seemed to be completely ignorant of the "fact" that slaves were captured, kidnapped
and brought to America in shackles. West immediately replied, "Of course I know that
slaves did not get shackled and put on a boat by free will." West also tweeted that
"the reason why I brought up the 400 years point is because we can't be mentally
imprisoned for another 400 years." (Twitter, May 1). West includes "mental
imprisonment" as a way that a person is enslaved, and through discussion and
dissent, we have the more credible opinion that "we can't be *mentally imprisoned* for
another 400 years." Perhaps West's revisions to his original claim are part of what
Mill means by a "portion of the truth" being released from the collision of alternative
opinions.

Second, we might question whether persons are always "improved" when they are convinced that an opinion that they once believed was false has been proved to be true. Suppose an individual always believed that 6 million Jews were murdered by the Nazi regime in Germany before and during WWII. This terrible event is called "the holocaust." And yet despite the evidence from a multitude of holocaust survivors, newspaper reports, films made of life in the camps, Nazi records of mass killings and burials, there are people referred to as "holocaust deniers" who believe that there was no holocaust. Mill would say that the belief of the holocaust denier is an example of an opinion that "might be true," and there is no justification for silencing an opinion that falls in this category. Why? Because in the *highly unlikely* but logically possible circumstance that the opinion of the holocaust denier is found to be true, individuals will have the opportunity to exchange error for truth and this exchange is always conducive to their mental well-being. If given a choice between P and not-P, and not-P is true, we should go with not-P, no matter how fervently and how long we had believed that P was true.

7.5 Objections and replies

Mill answers objections to each of the reasons (A) – (D), cited in 7.4. I will discuss two of the objections here.

7.5.1 *Censorship is not a declaration of infallibility*

To the first reason (A) for absolute freedom of opinion and expression, it might be objected that government restrictions on the propagation of erroneous opinions does not imply infallibility any more than it is implied by any other conduct of government. Government censors, like other government functionaries, must act on what they believe to be a true or false opinion. They are not assuming infallibility in this conduct any more than the elections clerk is assuming infallibility when she tallies the vote on a bill before the state legislature. No matter how many times she counts the vote, the elections clerk must eventually publish the count. And (by analogy) so must the censor act when a decision must be made about the truth of his opinion.

Mill replies that there is a world of difference between a government censor (or any government official who censors speech) and the conduct of other government officials. The elections clerk is assuming that her opinion on the voting results is true because, "with every opportunity for contesting it, it has not been refuted." But the censor makes no such assumption. He is assuming his opinion to be true, not because it has not yet been refuted, but "for the purpose of *not permitting* its refutation" (18).

7.5.2 *Christian morality is not the whole truth on the subject of morality*

A common objection is that *"some received principles, especially on the highest and most vital subjects, are more than half-truths. The Christian morality, for instance, is the whole truth on the subject, and if anyone teaches a morality which varies from it, he is wholly in error."* (46)

Although this objection has been met in 7.4, Mill's response is first, to "decide what is meant by Christian morality" (46). What he finds is that it is a morality that "has all the characters of a reaction; it is, in great part, a protest against paganism":

> Its ideal is negative rather than positive; passive rather than active; innocence rather than nobleness; abstinence from evil rather than energetic pursuit of good; in its precepts (as has been well said), "thou shalt not" predominates unduly over "thou shalt." ...It is essentially a doctrine of passive obedience. (47)

Mill also remarks that these features cannot be insinuated out of "the doctrines and precepts of Christ himself." (48) And yet even the sayings of Christ *"contain, and were meant to contain, only a part of the truth; that many of the essential elements of the highest morality are among the things which are not provided for, in the recorded deliverances of the Founder of Christianity."*

Therefore, the claim that Christian morals are the whole truth is "a pretension made by [it being only] a part of the truth."

> *If Christians would teach infidels to be just to Christianity, they should themselves be just to infidelity. It can do truth no service to blink the fact, known to all who have the most ordinary acquaintance with literary history, that a large portion of the noblest and most valuable moral teaching has been the work, not only of men who did not know, but of men who knew and rejected, the Christian faith. (49)*

The following quote appears to support Mill's point about who has bragging rights about the origin of moral teaching:

> Greece produced a line of unsurpassed moralists, a strange mystery to Christians for whom there is only one ethical route in the whole universe. Socrates and Plato believed in one God and were highly moral idealists. Athens was not so much the city of vice as the greatest morality making center the world has ever known. It culminated in the Stoic School which produced Christ-like austere moralists such as Epictetus and Marcus Aurelius and gave many educated Romans a high moral character. ... For one hundred and fifty years, Rome had Stoic emperors whose ethical level exceeded any in the history of Christendom. Of the twenty-nine Pagan Roman emperors twenty-one were admirable men of good character. (Magee, 2005)

7.6 Questions for thought and discussion

1. Is the United Kingdom justified in criminalizing hate speech? Is Germany justified in criminalizing speech that denies the holocaust?

2. Is it justifiable for government to compel so-called crisis pregnancy centers, which exist primarily to dissuade women from having abortions, to display prominent advertisements detailing the availability of state-funded abortions?

3. Should the U.S. Congress pass a law that creates an individual "right to be forgotten," by requiring Google and other search engines to delete any content about a person that is "irrelevant or no longer relevant"?

4. What restrictions, if any, should be placed on an adult's choice to purchase and read pornographic books or view pornographic videos? Does the publication of pornography violate the harm-to-others principle?

5. Members of the Old Order Amish religion and the Conservative Amish Mennonite Church sincerely believe that sending their children to school beyond the age of 15 is contrary to the Amish religion and way of life, and that this will endanger their own salvation and that of their children. How would Mill respond to this practice? Can the harm-to-others principle be used to justify the parental practice of not exposing their children to alternative religions or to atheism?

References

Abrams, Floyd. May 2, 2018. When 2 + 2 might equal 5. *New York Times.* https://nyti.ms/2KEmq6p

Amatulli, J. May 1, 2018. Kanye West calls slavery A 'choice,' gets schooled on history. *Huffington Post.* https://www.huffingtonpost.com/entry/kanye-west-slavery-tmz_us_5ae8c54ce4b00f70f0ecc118

Legal Dictionary. 2018. Hate speech. https://legaldictionary.net/hate-speech/

Liptak, Adam. 13 November 2017. Justices take cases on free speech at pregnancy centers and polling places. *New York Times.* https://www.nytimes.com/2017/11/13/us/politics/supreme-court-first-amendment-pregnancy-voting.html

Magee, M.D. 2005. Greece and Rome—Hellenism and Christianity. *Christianity.* http://www.askwhy.co.uk/christianity/0085HellenisticBG.php

Newth, Mette. 2010. The long history of censorship. *Beacon for Freedom of Expression.* http://www.beaconforfreedom.org/liste.html?tid=415&art_id=475

Plantinga, Alvin. 1983. Reason and belief in God, in *Faith and Rationality.* ed. A. Plantinga and N. Wolterstorff. Notre Dame, Indiana: University of Notre Dame Press.

Weiner, J. 30 August 2017. Fired professor: Hurricane Harvey 'karma ' tweet a 'heartbreaking' mistake. *Orlando Sentinel.*

http://www.orlandosentinel.com/news/politics/political-pulse/os-kenneth-storey-hurricane-harvey-apology-20170830-story.html

Chapter 8 Individuality (*On Liberty* III)

Do the reasons given in the previous chapter for the conclusion that individuals ought to be free to form opinions and to express their opinions also require that they ought to be *free to act* upon their opinions? Ought they to be free *"to act out in their lives without hindrance, either physical or moral, from their fellow men, so long as it is at their own risk or peril"*?

8.1 Examples of acting upon one's opinion

Let's begin with some examples of both historical and recent cases of men and women who have acted upon or been prevented from acting upon their opinion.

- Luis Andrew Martinez, also known as the "Naked Guy," acted on his opinion that clothes are "a symbol of elitism and repression" by walking naked on campus and to class at the University of California, Berkeley. (Goldston, 2006). He was eventually expelled from the university and arrested in the city of Berkeley on misdemeanor charges of public nudity.
- A white student at a California state university wore blackface during a fraternity costume party (Branson-Potts, 2018). The student apologized and said that he did not know about the one-hundred-year history of the use of blackface as a way of humiliating black Americans (*Blackface!* 2018). No charges were brought against him.
- Waving Confederate flags, chanting Nazi-era slogans, wearing helmets and carrying shields, white nationalists converged on the Robert E. Lee statue inside a Charlottesville, Virginia park on and began chanting phrases like "You will not replace us" and "Jews will not replace us" (Stolberg and Rosenthal).
- A group of American University students burned U.S. flags on the Washington D.C. campus to protest Donald Trump's election as president on November 8, 2016, some shouting "F— white America!" (Svrluga and Matos).
- In 2001 a woman was fired from her job at a car rental company in Phoenix, AZ, for refusing to remove her hijab (headscarf) during the Muslim holy month of Ramadan, despite the fact that she was wearing it in accordance with her religious beliefs (American Civil Liberties Union). She successfully sued the car company for damages.

8.2 Experiments in living and limitations on individuality

Mill writes that although individuals should be free to act upon their opinions, "no one pretends that actions should be as free as opinions" (53). Merely having an opinion or expressing it to others orally or in writing does no harm to others, except in those circumstances in which the expression is "a positive instigation to some mischievous act" (53). The example Mill gives of a *positive instigation* is shouting the words "Corn dealers are starvers of the poor!" to an excited mob assembled before the house of a corn dealer.

> The term "to incite a riot", or "to organize, promote, encourage, participate in, or carry on a riot", includes, but is not limited to, urging or instigating other persons to riot, but shall not be deemed to mean the mere oral or written (1) advocacy of ideas or (2) expression of belief, not involving advocacy of any act or acts of violence or assertion of the rightness of, or the right to commit, any such act or acts. (18 U.S. Code, §2102 – Definitions)

Although is not clear whether Mill means that this oral expression is mere opinion or a kind of action, he uses the corn dealer example to make a larger point about the justifiable limits that can be placed on a physical expression of individuality. The limitation is "acts *of any kind* which without justifiable cause do harm to others."

> *The liberty of the individual must be thus far limited; he must not make himself a nuisance to other people. But if he refrains from molesting others in what, concerns them and merely acts according to his own inclination and judgment in things which concern himself, the same reasons which show that opinion should be free prove also that he should be allowed, without molestation, to carry his opinions into practice at his own cost. (53)*

Mill's limitation requirement appears to be identical to the harm-to-others principle (6.2), with the exception that Mill now adds behavior like "make himself a nuisance to others," and "molesting others" to his list of ways of doing harm to others.

But if a physical expression of an opinion does no harm to others (for example, wearing a hijab to work), then (to repeat what was quoted above) "...the same reasons which show that opinion should be free [also] prove also that he should be allowed to carry his opinions into practice at his own cost" (53). Those reasons are:

> *Mankind are not infallible; that their truths for the most part, are only half-truths; that unity of opinion, unless resulting from the fullest and freest comparison of opposite opinions, is not desirable and diversity not an evil, but a good...*
>
> *[T]here should be different experiments of living; that free scope should be given to varieties of character, short of injury to others; and that the worth of different modes of life should be proved physically, when anyone thinks fit to try them. It is desirable, in short, that in things which do not primarily concern others, individuality should assert itself. (54).*

Mill is convinced that experiments in living in which there is a free development of individuality, "is one of the leading essentials of well-being" (54).

He who lets the world, or his own portion of it, choose his plan of life for him has no need of any other faculty than the ape-like one of imitation. He who chooses his plan for himself employs all his faculties. He must use observation to see, reasoning and judgment to foresee, activity to gather materials for decision, discrimination to decide, and when he has decided, firmness and self-control to hold to his deliberate decision (56).

8.3 The well-developed human being

The end result of cultivating individuality is "the well-developed human being." This implies a standard of human development that allows us to rank human beings as more or less developed, with "poorly developed" at the bottom and "well developed" at the top. Unfortunately, Mill does not provide the details of a standard, but perhaps one can be extracted from relevant passages in the book. The first passage is the one just cited. A well-developed person is one who "chooses a plan for himself." In more contemporary language, she is a completely autonomous human being. A poorly developed person is one who is not autonomous at all. She will simply imitate the plan of others. Second, the well-developed person is one who has "the highest and most harmonious development of his powers [put] into a complete and consistent whole" (55, quoting Humboldt). Third, the powers which the well-developed person must possess are "the human faculties of perception, judgment, discriminative feeling, mental activity, and even moral preference" (56). A less well-developed person will either lack one or more of these powers, or if she has them all, will not have placed them in harmony with each other. Fourth, the well-developed person does not do a thing merely because others do it, nor will she believe a thing merely because others believe it. She disdains custom.

8.4 Hard cases

Looking back at the examples of "acting upon one's opinion" (8.1), the question we should ask in each case is whether the individual has violated the harm-to-others principle.

Each case is a challenge because of the vagueness of the term "harm." If being harmed means being *physically hurt* (injured, in pain), then none of the actions in the examples caused harm. The naked guy, the woman wearing the hijab, the student who wore blackface, and the students who burned American flags have this much in common: no one was harmed because no one was physically hurt.

But suppose that we extend the word "harm" to mean "*emotional pain*". In that case, we would probably find many persons who say they were offended and distressed when they saw the U.S. flag being burned. Many students on campus reported distress when they learned about the blackface incident, and hundreds of counter-protesters at Charlottesville said that they were deeply offended by the expression of hatred expressed by the white nationalist marchers against non-white minorities and Jews. Some of the people on the University of California campus who saw the naked guy for the first time as he walked directly toward them, felt *shock* and *embarrassment*.

Mill appears to widen the concept of harm to include emotional pain when he mentions how a person expressing his or her individuality might be a "nuisance" to others. When we use this word to describe the behavior of others, we are reporting our own negative feelings. Thus, if people says that the naked guy is a nuisance, they mean that his behavior "annoys" or "disgusts" them.

> Mill also uses the word "molesting" as a synonym for harming, although he does not use it to mean what this word has come to mean in the twenty-first century. The verb "to molest," for Mill and others in the nineteenth-century means "to bother or annoy" not "to harm through sexual contact."

Mill uses the word "interest" in discussing harm to others. Thus, harming another means doing something that "concerns the interests of other people" (10). In this case, a great deal will depend on what constitutes an "interest" and whether all or only some interests that are "of concern" ought to count as harmful. For example, everyone has an interest in staying alive, being healthy and free from physical and emotional pain, an interest in protecting their family from the same, protecting one's reputation in the community, and so on.

But what is included in the "so on"? Should we include the supervisor who fired the employee who wore a hijab to work? What interest of his was affected? He might argue that he has an interest in the profitability of his car rental company, and fears that he will suffer monetary losses if people with anti-Muslin beliefs refuse to rent his cars. In other words, this woman's behavior "concerns the interests" of the supervisor.

We now have several different ways of causing harm to others. Everyone agrees that causing physical hurt to another constitutes harm. The debate and confusion are about whether harm constitutes more than this. Here is a list (with page numbers) that includes everything that Mill has explicitly mentioned in *On Liberty* as variations of doing harm to others:

- Producing evil to others by one's action (9)
- Producing evil to others by one's inaction (11)
- Acting in ways that concerns the interests of others (10)
- An act [that is] hurtful to others (10)
- Being a nuisance to others (53)
- Molesting others (53)
    To this list we should add two other variants:
- Causing emotional pain to others

- Causing offense to others

If you are confused by this list of synonyms for the word "harm," your confusion is justifiable. The kinds of actions that constitute harm to others appears to encompass almost everything we do in everyday life. Most of what we do concerns the interests of others in some way or other, and a great deal of what persons do in political or religious activity might be a nuisance to others, cause them emotional pain or offend them. The question is: where do we draw the line? At what point can it be truly said that we have caused harm to others, with the implication that our conduct is eligible for either social or legal sanctions, or both? Mill answers this question in the next chapter.

8.5 Questions for thought and discussion

1. How does Mill's description of the well-developed human being fit into his utilitarian theory? Is it consistent with the principle of utility?

2. What is individuality? What does individuality have to do with the utilitarian theory of life?

3. Of the examples of individuality noted in section 8.1, which one presents the least problem for the harm-to-others principle? Which one presents the greatest problem? Explain.

4. What would Mill do about entire communities of people, bound together by their religious beliefs, who would strongly resist any effort to "liberate" their children from their way of life by exposing them to ways of life in other religious communities? Is there a way to justify this kind of parental resistance? (For further information on the clash between the efforts of a state to require children to attend high school and parental efforts to keep them in their community during these formative years, see the U.S Supreme Court's decision and reasoning on this issue in *Wisconsin v. Yoder*, 406 U.S. 205 (1972).

References

American Civil Liberties Union. 2018. Discrimination against Muslim women – fact sheet, fn. 1 and 12. https://www.aclu.org/other/discrimination-against-muslim-women-fact-sheet#12

Blackface! 2018. History of blackface. http://black-face.com/

Branson-Potts, Hailey. 2018. After blackface incident, minority students at Cal Poly San Luis Obispo say they don't feel welcome. *Los Angeles Times*. April 25, 2018. http://www.latimes.com/local/lanow/la-me-cal-poly-slo-blackface-20180504-story.html

Carmichael, Sarah Green. 2017. Study: Employers are less likely to hire a woman who wears a headscarf. *Harvard Business Review.* https://hbr.org/2017/05/study-employers-are-less-likely-to-hire-a-woman-who-wears-a-headscarf. May 26, 2017.

Goldston, Linda. 2006 and 2016. Berkeley 'naked guy' had a charismatic life and a tragic death. *East Bay Times.* https://www.eastbaytimes.com/2006/11/15/berkeley-naked-guy-had-charismatic-life-and-a-tragic-death-2/

Ipsos-Mori. 2017. Three in four women around the world believe there are unequal rights in their country. https://www.ipsos.com/ipsos-mori/en-uk/three-four-women-around-world-believe-there-are-unequal-rights-their-country

Mill, John Stuart. *The Subjection of Women.* London, 1869.

PBS News Hour. 2015. Why we think the way we do about men, women and work. https://www.pbs.org/newshour/nation/the-lasting-impact-of-the-plow-on-our-attitudes-about-gender-and-work January 5, 2015.

Sharp-Wasserman, Julio. Happiness and individuality in Mill. *Pharmakon Journal of Philosophy 3rd issue* (no date). https://american.edu/cas/philrel/pdf/upload/Sharp-Wasserman.pdf

Stolberg, Sheryl Gay and Brian M. Rosenthal. Man charged after white nationalist rally in Charlottesville ends in deadly violence. *New York Times.* August 12, 2017. https://www.nytimes.com/2017/08/12/us/charlottesville-protest-white-nationalist.html?rref=collection%2Fbyline%2Fsheryl-gay-stolberg&action=click&contentCollection=undefined&region=stream&module=stream_unit&version=latest&contentPlacement=21&pgtype=collection

Svrluga, Susan and Alejandro Matos. Student protesters burn American flags at confrontation over Trump victory. *Washington Post.* November 9, 2016. https://www.washingtonpost.com/news/grade-point/wp/2016/11/09/student-protesters-burn-american-flags-at-confrontation-over-trump-victory/?noredirect=on&utm_term=.0e1134d924dc

The Week. 2018. Six things women in Saudi Arabia cannot do. *Weekday Newsletter.* April 10, 2018. http://www.theweek.co.uk/60339/things-women-cant-do-in-saudi-arabia

Wisconsin v. Yoder, 406 U.S. 205 (1972).

Chapter 9 Society and the Individual (*On Liberty* IV)

In the opening paragraph of chapter IV Mill repeats the question that he first asked in Chapter I.

> What, then, is the rightful limit to the sovereignty of the individual over himself? Where does the authority of society begin? How much of human life should be assigned to individuality, and how much to society? (73)

He gives an immediate answer to these questions in the next paragraph, although he uses the same vague language in this answer as he provided in the first formulation of the harm-to-others principle.

> Each will receive its proper share if each has that which more particularly concerns it. To individuality belong the part of life in which it is chiefly the individual that is interested; to society, the part which chiefly interests society. (73)

And we are still left with the same questions. What does Mill mean by the words "concern" and "interests"? How are we to determine whether a part of one's life concerns others or chiefly interests society?

To our great relief, Mill comes to the rescue in the third paragraph by making a significant revision to the original harm-to-others principle. The line of conduct that everyone who lives in society should be bound to observe consists,

> First, in not injuring the interests of one another, or rather certain interests which, either by express legal provision or by tacit understanding, ought to be considered as rights; and secondly, in each persons' bearing his share (to be fixed on some equitable principle) of the labors and sacrifices incurred for defending the society or its members from injury and molestation. (73)

The game-changing phrase here is "interests which ought to be considered as rights." For example, I have an interest in parking at a favorite spot located close to my university office, but I *have no right* to park there, and other persons are not "bound to restrain themselves" from parking there. I also have an interest that no one hits me over the head when I get out of my car. I *have a right* not to be assaulted by anyone, and all persons are bound to restrain themselves from acts of assault on others.

Mill makes the additional point that there are many acts that are "hurtful or wanting in due consideration for the welfare of others, but do not violate any of their constituted rights." Acts of this kind should only be "punished by opinion...not by law." I see that my favorite parking spot is open, but I also see that a recently injured colleague who must use crutches to get around is also headed for that spot. I get to the spot before him and quickly park my car. I did not violate any right of his, but my behavior is certainly insensitive and worthy of blame, although not legally punishable.

9.1 Harm to others as a violation of rights

The harm principle is revised, the notion of "a right" is reintroduced, and we now learn that there are two types of rights involved in the second formulation of the harm principle.

9.1.1 A new version of the harm principle

The first version of the harm-to-others principle (HOP) says that society is justified in limiting individual liberty when liberty is used to cause harm to others. Let's now call this HOP1 The second version replaces the phrase "harm to others" with the lengthier phrase "injuries to those interests which ought to be considered as rights." Thus, the only harms that are protectable by law and opinion are those interests *which ought to be considered as rights.* We'll call this HOP2.

9.1.2 The concept of "a right"

In *Utilitarianism*, Mill defines "a right," as a "valid claim on society to protect him [the right-holder] in the possession of it, either by force of law or by that of education and opinion" (52). For example, if someone claims that they have a *right to liberty*, the claim is valid only if it is true that society ought to come to the defense of persons whose liberty is in jeopardy.

When someone has a claim-right of any kind three parties are involved: the right-holder, actual or potential offenders (those who do or might interfere with an exercise of the right) and society. The valid claim that the right-holder is making is *against society itself*, namely that society ought to use the force of law or the force of public opinion to defend and protect the right-holder against any offender.

The idea of a right marks the distinction between doing an injustice to another and a failure to be generous to another. It also marks the distinction between injuries to interests considered as violations of rights and injuries to interests that are not considered as violations of rights. If someone steals money from a beggar's tin cup, then he has violated the beggar's right to possess the money. But if someone refuses a request to donate money to the beggar, she does not violate a right of the beggar. Although the beggar has an interest in obtaining the money, she has no valid claim to it (assuming that no promises or other agreements had previously been made to this effect).

9.1.3 Two types of rights

Mill makes or implies a distinction between two kinds of rights: *constituted rights* and *rights that derive from distinct and assignable obligations.* The adjective "constituted" means "established by law." Thus, the rights to life and liberty are "constituted" rights because established laws exist prohibiting assaults on a person's life or liberty. These rights are universal, applying to everyone.

The words "distinct and assignable obligations" refer to the obligations of particular persons in special roles. Mill's examples are a police officer, a parent, and a borrower of money (79). The police officer has a special duty to protect the public from harm, a parent has a special duty to care for and protect her children, and the borrower has a special obligation to pay back the loan he received from the creditor. In each case, the obligation generates a correlative right to a distinct person or group of persons – the public, children, creditors. These rights can be violated. The police officer might fail to protect the public. The father might abandon his children, and the borrower might fail to pay off his loan.

9.2 Testing HOP2

HOP2 provides a way out of the confusion encountered in HOP1 by the large number of synonyms Mill had earlier used to define the idea of harm. We now know from HOP2 that the only *protectable* harms or interests of others are those which constitute a person's constituted rights or distinct and assignable rights (that is, rights derived from distinction and assignable obligations).

Turning now to the cases described in the previous chapter, the question to ask is whether the individual's conduct was such as to violate another's right. In the case of the naked guy at U.C. Berkeley, he did no harm to others because he did not violate anyone's right in the year 1992 on the campus of U.C. Berkeley or in the city of Berkeley, because in that year there was no university or city statute making this conduct illegal. However, in the next year (1993), both the university administration and the city council made public nudity a misdemeanor, giving persons the constituted right not to involuntarily confront nude people in public places.

Two other cases described at 3.1 can be dealt with quickly. The man who wore blackface and the Muslim woman who wore her hijab to work did no harm to others for the same reason that the naked guy did no harm to others in the year 1992. They did not violate any interests of others that either are rights or ought to be considered as rights. In the U.S., there are constitutional protections for the actions of the blackface man and the Muslim woman.

The 2017 white nationalist demonstration in Charlottesville, Virginia is more complicated. There was a large, organized contingent of counter-demonstrators who had gathered there. Some people carried weapons. Many people were injured in the ensuing riots. One of the white nationalists drove into a group of counter-demonstrators, killing a young woman and injuring another nineteen demonstrators. A police helicopter crashed, killing two police officers Although the white nationalists had obtained the necessary permits for their demonstration, there were some who accused them of instigating the riot. Others accused the counter-demonstrators of the instigation. (Neier, 2017).

Comparisons have been made between the 2017 white nationalist march in Charlottesville and a 1977 march proposed a small group of neo-Nazis in Skokie, Illinois. The latter march was to take place down a street of homes occupied primarily by Jews, including some who had lived through the holocaust. The Skokie march was held up for fifteen months by a lawsuit that eventually went to the U.S. Supreme Court. The Court ruled that the neo-Nazis had a constitutional right to march, but the march never took place on the assigned date (Neier, 2017).

9.3 Rights and general utility

There is a logical fallacy known as "begging the question." The fallacy occurs when a person asks a question that assumes an affirmative answer has been given to a previous question. Thus, if one man asks another "Have you stopped beating your children?" he assumes that the man has previously admitted to beating his children. The assumption might be false.

Those who insist that the naked guy, the blackface student, the Muslim woman, and the white nationalist marchers did *not* violate the harm-to-others principle, using HOP2 as their test, might be accused of begging the important question "*Ought* they have a right to do what they did?" Those who defend these people are assuming that an affirmative answer has previously been given to this question. But has it?

In the U.S., the assumption can be defended by reference to the rights guaranteed under the U.S. Constitution. If it is asked whether the Charlottesville marchers *ought* to have the right to demonstrate on that tragic day in Charlottesville, it would seem that this question is affirmatively answered by reference to the First Amendment. But even then, the answer might be challenged because the First Amendment only protects the right "*peaceably* to assemble." Many of the white nationalists arrived for their demonstration in Charlottesville heavily armed.

If it asked whether the naked guy *ought* to have the right to be naked in public, it may be troublesome that he had this right in 1992 but lost it in 1993, after the U.C. Berkeley administrators and the Berkeley city council made public nudity illegal. But we can still ask the question "*Ought* this right be granted to the public?"

Mill is quite aware that this question will be asked. In *Utilitarianism*, after declaring that having a right is to have something which society *ought* to defend me in the possession of, Mill writes: "if the objector goes on to ask why it ought, I can give him no other reason than general utility" (*Util.*, 52). Thus, in deciding whether persons ought to have the right to doff their clothes in public, the Berkeley city council probably used some degree of utilitarian thinking by weighing the consequences of allowing public nudity against the consequences of prohibiting it. They would have decided that the bad consequence of involuntarily confronting a naked stranger outweighed the good consequence of not interfering with those who enjoy being naked in public.

9.4 Objections to the revised harm-to-self principle

One of the objections to the first version of the harm-to-others principle (HOP1) is that it declares that harm to others is the *only* justification for limiting an individual's liberty. This implies that conduct which harms only oneself is *never* a justification for legal or moral intervention.

HOP2 does not change this implication. HOP2 narrows the concept of harm to include only those harms or injuries to the interests of others that ought to be considered as rights, but this has no effect on the notion of harm to oneself. It still remains the case that there is *no justification* for interfering with a person's liberty if the only reason for the interference is that this will be good for her or it will prevent her from doing harm to herself.

Mill is aware of the objections to HOP1, some of which he mentioned (6.8) but deferred his replies until now, perhaps because he was looking ahead to HOP2 and a stronger case that could be made for the conclusion that society ought never to interfere with conduct that harms or risks harm only to oneself. Some of this case has previously been made when Mill rejected harm to oneself as a viable liberty limiting principle (6.3.1). His aim in these pages is to take another look at the reasons that have been given for justifying HSP.

9.4.1 It is selfish indifference to ignore the good of others

Mill's hypothetical objector:

> ...[I]t is... selfish indifference [to] pretend that human beings have no business with each other's conduct in life, and that they should not concern themselves about the well-doing or well-being of one another, unless their own interest is involved. (74)

Mill's reply:

> Human beings owe to each other help to distinguish the better from the worse, and encouragement to choose the latter, and encouragement to choose the former and avoid the latter...But neither one person nor any number of persons, is warranted in saying to another creature of ripe years that he shall not do with his life for his own benefit what he chooses to do with it.

Mill's reasons:

> First, "he is the person most interested in his own well-being: the interest which any other person, except in cases of strong personal attachment [spouse, parents, siblings], can have in it is trifling compared with that which he himself has." (74)

Second, *"the interference of society to overrule his judgment and purposes in what only regard himself must be grounded on general presumptions which may be altogether wrong and, even if right, are as likely as not to be misapplied to individual cases, by persons no better acquainted with the circumstances of such cases than those are who look at them merely from without."* (74)

There are many examples of situations in which local legislators have made general presumptions about the good of the citizens, whether it be about their health or the way they choose to live. In New York city an ordinance was passed prohibiting the sale of oversize soda drinks containing sugar. The noble objective was to combat obesity. In some U.S. cities ordinances have been passed prohibiting cars parked on front lawns, and trash cans left at curbside after weekly pick-up (the cans should be placed out of public sight). Perhaps the car and trash can cases are tied to an alleged right not to have the public's "aesthetic sensibilities" offended.

9.4.2 No person is an isolated being

Mill's hypothetical objector:

First, "the distinction here pointed out between the part of a person's life which concerns only himself and that which concerns others, many persons will refuse to admit. How (it may be asked) can any part of the conduct of a member of society be a matter of indifference to the other members? No person is an isolated being." (78)

Second, an individual who *"injur[es] his property"* thereby harms those who directly or indirectly derive support from it; if he *"deteriorates his bodily or mental faculties"* he brings evil upon all who depended upon him for any portion of their happiness; and finally, if by his vices or follies he does no direct harm to others, he may be *"injurious by his example,"* and ought to be compelled to control himself for the sake of others whom the sight or knowledge of his conduct might corrupt or mislead." (78)

Third, if it is justifiable to protect children and persons under age, then society should be "equally bound" to protect "persons who are equally incapable of self-government," for example, by prohibiting gambling, drunkenness, incontinence, idleness or uncleanliness, all of which are "as injurious to unhappiness, and as great a hindrance to improvement as many or most of the acts prohibited by law." (78)

Mill's replies:

To the first and second objection: Mill admits that *"the mischief which a person does to himself may seriously affect"* his family friends, and to a lesser degree, "society at large." But the words "seriously affect" do not add up to a protectable harm. As previously noted (4.1.2), harms are protectable (by law or opinion) only when they either derive from a *constituted right* or a *right that derives from a distinct and assignable obligation.*

The examples that Mill uses are (1) "a man who, through intemperance or extravagance, becomes unable to pay his debts," or (2) who, having undertaken the responsibility of a family, becomes incapable of supporting or educating them; or (3) a soldier or policeman who is drunk on duty.

The general point Mill is making is that each of these men *"might be justly punished; but it is for the breach of duty to his family or creditors [or to the public], not for the extravagance,"* that is, *not for being drunk.*

The duty breached is the "distinct and assignable obligation" referred to above. When this obligation is breached, "the case is taken out of the self-regarding class and becomes amenable to moral disapprobation in the proper sense of the term... Whenever, in short, there is a definite damage, or a definite risk of damage, either to an individual or the public, the case is taken out of the province of liberty and placed in that of morality or law." (79-80)

> But with regard to the merely contingent or, as it may be called the constructive injury which a person causes to society by conduct which neither violates any specific duty to the public, nor occasions perceptible hurt to any assignable individual except himself, the inconvenience is one which society can afford to bear, for the sake of the greater good of human freedom. (80)

As to the objection that society should be protected from persons who set "bad examples" for others, Mill observes that "we are speaking of conduct which is supposed to do great damage to the agent himself." Surely if the damage the person is doing to himself is known to others, then the example is "good," not bad. It does far more to discourage rather than encourage others to imitate him.

> Anyone who has seen the shocking anti-smoking videos of former smokers battling throat and lung cancer would certainly be discouraged from taking up the habit. The example they set for others is good, not bad. https://www.youtube.com/watch?v=5zWB4dLYChM

To the third objection, Mill replies that the objector wrongly assumes that society has done little or nothing to prevent persons from being incapable of self-government when they reach the age of reason.

> Society has had absolute power over them during all the early portion of their existence; it has had the whole period of childhood and nonage in which to try whether it could make them capable of rational conduct in life... If society lets any considerable number of its members grow up mere children, incapable of being acted on by rational consideration of distant motives, society has itself to blame for the consequences. (80)

Moreover, Mill adds, there is always the considerable chance that if society attempts to prohibit an adult from engaging in what it believes is "irrational" self-regarding conduct, "they will infallibly rebel against the yoke... It easily comes to be considered a mark of spirit and courage to fly in the face of such usurped authority and do with ostentation the exact opposite of what it enjoins" (81).

Mill's reasons:

> ...the strongest of all the arguments against the interference of the public with purely personal conduct is that, when it does interfere, the odds are that it interferes wrongly and in the wrong place (81).

On questions about our duty to others (social morality), the majority, "though often wrong, is likely to be still oftener, right "because on such questions they are only required to judge of their own interests, of the manner in which some mode of conduct, if allowed to be practiced, would affect themselves." If asked whether we have or ought to have a duty to restrain ourselves from breaking promises or contracts, telling lies, or causing physical harm to others, we are likely to be right about these restraints because we are asked to think about how *we would like it* if we were the victims of such conduct.

It is otherwise with self-regarding conduct,

> ...for in these cases public opinion means, at the best, some people's opinion of what is good or bad for other people, while very often it does not mean even that—the public, with the most perfect indifference, passing over the pleasure or convenience of those whose conduct they censure and considering only their own preference. (81)

If asked whether smoking marijuana should be legally prohibited, the U.S. public generally and for many years did not consider that many citizens enjoyed smoking and ingesting marijuana. It was enough for a majority to declare that they did not prefer it (although they did prefer alcohol), and that was all that mattered. Their representatives in legislative bodies, until recently, voted accordingly (Siff, 2014).

9.5 Mid-nineteenth century examples of the "moral police"

When Mill uses the phrase "moral police" he means "the public of this age and country [who] improperly invests its own preference with the character of moral laws." Mill gives examples of this practice to show that the harm-to-others principle "is of serious and practical moment, and that I am not endeavoring to erect a barrier against imaginary evils."

> And it is not difficult to show, by abundant instances, that to extend the bounds of what may be called moral police until it encroaches on the most unquestionably legitimate liberty of the individual is one of the most universal of all propensities. (82)

Here is an incomplete list of Mill's "instances." I recommend but will not here analyze his critical discussion of each example. But let us remember that Mill regards nothing he writes, whether positive or negative, as "the whole truth."

- The Christian and European moral abhorrence of the Muslim religious practice of not eating pork, a meat that they call "unclean." Mill remarks that "the only tenable ground of condemnation would be that with the personal tastes and self-regarding concerns of individuals the public has no business to interfere." (83)
- No other religion than the Roman Catholic is lawful in Spain. Mill warns that "unless we are willing to adopt the logic of persecutors, and to say that *we* may persecute others because we are right, and that *they* must not persecute us because they are wrong, we must beware of admitting a principle of which we should resent as a gross injustice the application to ourselves." (84)
- "Wherever the Puritans have been sufficiently powerful, as in New England, and Great Britain at the time of the Commonwealths, they have endeavored, with considerable success, to put down all public, and nearly all private, amusements, especially music, dancing, public games or other assemblages for the purpose of diversion, and the theater" (84). Mill asked what would happen if an even stricter religion came along that forbids the few amusements that are permitted to the Puritans. "Would they not...desire these intrusively pious members of society to mind their own business?" (85).

9.6 Questions for thought and discussion

1. Should there be a right not to be harmed which would include harming oneself? Can a credible case be made for the claim that when Vincent van Gogh intentionally cut off his ear he violated an obligation not to harm himself? What would be the origin of this obligation?

2. The reader should note that many of Mill's reasons for rejecting self-regarding harms as a justification for limiting personal liberty are *empirical judgments*. These are the kind of judgment that must be supported by observation, experiment, data and

other kinds of relevant evidence. What evidence for his empirical judgments does Mill provide?

3. There are a great many paternalistic laws in the U.S. that restrict self-regarding conduct, for example, laws requiring people to wear seat-belts when driving a car or to obtain a prescription before they can purchase certain drugs for their ailments. How would Mill apply HOP2 to these laws?

4. At 6.3.2 and 6.3.3 two liberty-limiting principles were described to show that there are other categories of non-harmful conduct which have been made illegal: conduct that is generally believed to be *immoral* and conduct that is *offensive*. Can a case be made for limiting the liberty of individuals for the reason that their conduct, although not harmful to others (HOP2), is either immoral or offensive?

References

Neier, Aryeh. 2017. Skokie and Charlottesville: why even neo-Nazi speech needs to be protected. *Newsweek, U.S. Edition.* October 22, 2017. http://www.newsweek.com/skokie-and-charlottesville-why-even-neo-nazi-speech-needs-be-protected-690235.

Siff, Stephen. 2014. The illegalization of marijuana: a brief history. *Origins: Current Events in Historical Perspectives.* Vol. 7, issue 8. May 2014. http://origins.osu.edu/article/illegalization-marijuana-brief-history

Chapter 10 Applications (*On Liberty* V)

In the final chapter Mill gives several answers to "questions of details" about the two principles (maxims) asserted throughout the previous chapters. He does this by applying them to difficult cases and situations involving liberty and restraint. Mill's answers (as in the last chapter) not only allow the reader to think through examples of how the principles should be applied to real cases, but they help to clarify the principles themselves.

Mill begins by reminding us about the content of the two principles:

> *The maxims are, first, that the individual is not accountable to society for his actions in so far as these concern the interests of no person but himself. Advice, instruction, persuasion, and avoidance by other people, if thought necessary by them for their own good, are the only measures by which society can justifiably express its dislike or disapprobation of his conduct. Secondly, that for such actions as are prejudicial to the interests of others, the individual is accountable and may be subjected either to social or to legal punishment if society is of opinion that the one or the other is requisite for its protection. (93)*

The first of these maxims tells us that harm to oneself (HSP) *is not* a justifiable liberty-limiting principle. The second maxim tells us that *only* harm to others (HOP2) justifies limiting the liberty of individuals, either by law or by public opinion.

10.1 Trade, free trade and trade wars

Mill uses an application of HOP2 to the business of *trade* as a way of showing that there are some interests that are inevitably damaged in such competition, but which must be tolerated. When businesses are selling the same product, there will be winners and losers. If one tradesperson offers a lower price or a better product, then pain or loss will be suffered by those with whom she competes. But this is a legitimate win on her part.

> *...society admits no right, either legal or moral, in the disappointed competitors to immunity from this kind of suffering and feels called on to interfere only when means of success have been employed which it is contrary to the general interest to permit—namely, fraud or treachery, and force. (94);*

Mill writes that "trade is a social act," meaning that he who sells goods to the public "does what affects the interest of other persons, and of society in general; and thus, his conduct, in principle, comes within the jurisdiction of society." (94) The doctrine of "free trade," leaves producers and sellers perfectly free, "under the sole check of equal freedom to the buyers for supplying themselves elsewhere."

The principle of *individual* liberty (HOP2) is not involved in the doctrine of free trade. Nor is it involved in the limits of free trade, "for example, what amount of public control is admissible for the prevention of fraud by adulteration [food fraud]; how far sanitary precautions, or arrangements to protect workpeople employed in dangerous occupations, should be enforced on employers." Although these are interferences with the liberty of the producer or seller, they do not make it impossible or difficult for a *buyer* to obtain a particular commodity, at least as long as she has the freedom to buy the desired product elsewhere (95). Hence, competition for a share of the market is not in itself a violation of the harm-to-others principle.

"Free trade" is now defined as a policy which leaves international trade to its natural course without tariffs, quotas, or other restrictions. A "trade war" is a situation in which countries try to damage each other's trade, typically by the imposition of tariffs or quota restrictions.

10.2 Prevention of crime and accidents

No one denies that government has the prevention of crime as one of its most important obligations. It does this in two ways: preventing crime *before* it is committed and punishing it *after* it has been committed. The preventive function "is far more liable to be abused to the prejudice of liberty, than the primary function" because there are so many legitimate human actions which have the potential of becoming criminal or facilitating crime. (95)

Mill uses buying or using poisons as his example. There is nothing illegitimate about this activity. What makes it illegitimate is using poison (say) to commit a murder. If this were the only use of poisons, then society may interfere to prevent its manufacture and sale. "They may, however, be wanted not only for innocent but for useful purposes, and restrictions cannot be imposed in the one case without operating in the other." (95)

The "the case of the decrepit bridge," relevant to the second application, is one of the most quoted passages from *On Liberty*:

> If either a public officer or anyone else saw a person attempting to cross a bridge which had been ascertained to be unsafe, and there was no time to warn him of his danger, they might seize him and turn him back, without any real infringement on his liberty; for liberty consists in doing what one desires, and he does not desire to fall into the river. (95)

After making certain that he understands the risk, he is not a child, delirious or mentally impaired, and he still wants to cross the bridge, we cannot "forcibly prevent [him] from exposing himself [to the danger]."

The same kind of precaution can be used to resolve the poisons case. "[L]abelling the drug with some word expressive of its dangerous character may be enforced without violation of liberty: the buyer cannot wish not to know that the thing he possesses has poisonous qualities." (96)

Mill now admits that that there must be limitations to the maxim that "purely self-regarding conduct cannot be properly be meddled with in the way of prevention and punishment." The case that troubles him is the perpetual drunk.

> If he had once been convicted of any act of violence to others while drunk, he "should be placed under a special legal restriction; that if he was afterwards found drunk, he should be liable to a penalty, and that if, when in that state, he committed another offense, the punishment to which he would be liable for that other offense should be increased in severity. The making himself drunk, in a person whom drunkenness excites to do harm to others is a crime against others. (97)

10.3 Violations of good manners and standards of decency

There is a group of acts that are self-regarding but which, if done publicly, Mill recommends ought to be moved into the other-regarding category. These are acts which,

> ...being directly injurious only to the agents themselves, ought not to be legally interdicted, but which, if done publicly, are a violation of good manners and coming thus within the category of offenses against others, may rightly be prohibited. Of this kind are offenses against decency. (97, my emphasis)

This comes as quite a surprise, especially after having read the chapter IV on individuality. Isn't it possible that one might choose an "experiment in living" knowing full well that she is violating "good manners"? If so, why does Mill, at this final chapter in *On Liberty*, argue that this *kind* of experiment in living "may rightly be prohibited"?

In the preceding quote, Mill says that these experiments in living are directly injurious only to themselves." He gives no examples of "private injurious acts" that persons might also perform in public. Some commentators on Mill have said that he is probably thinking about consensual sexual intercourse (Lacewing, 4). My first thought was about the U.C. Berkeley naked guy. But it is difficult to understand how these behaviors are injurious to the persons who are having the intercourse or walking around nude, either in private or in public. Perhaps a better example is masturbation, which was once widely believed to be injurious to the masturbator. A more likely case would be the drunk or the glutton who not only harms himself, but drinks or eats so much that he vomits on a public sidewalk in full view of several pedestrians.

Indecent exposure laws in most states make it a crime to purposefully display one's genitals in public, causing others to be alarmed or offended. Indecent exposure is often committed for the sexual gratification of the offender or committed to entice a sexual response (FindLaw).

If Mill is appealing to HOP2, then he must think that violations of good manners are violations of a right (see the inset above). Perhaps Mill believes at this point that any indecent public act is other-regarding. This may be true, but only because "done in public" means "done in view of others." But how does Mill get from "done in view of others" to "may be prohibited"? On the harm-to-others principle (HOP2), it is only the violation of *those interests that qualify as individual rights* that may be legally prohibited. Therefore, it is the "indecency" component of the public act that allows Mill to get from "done in view of others" to "may be prohibited." This begs the question "Ought people have the right to not be exposed to indecent behavior when in public?"

10.4 Solicitations to do an immoral or illegal act

There is a class of acts which are not "strictly within the definition of individual liberty, yet the reasons on which the principle of individual liberty is grounded are applicable to it." This class includes soliciting by giving advice or inducements to engage in "blamable personal conduct," for example, fornication (prostitution) or gambling.

On first sight, we might want to blame or punish both the solicitor and the offender. But it is not within the definition of individual liberty that we should blame the solicitor. That definition includes not only freedom of action and expression, but it also includes the freedom "to consult with one another about what is fit to be so done; to exchange opinions and give and receive suggestions." (97). If we are permitted to gamble (at our own peril), then surely, we must be permitted to *advise others* to gamble (at their own peril).

But does the principle of individual liberty (HOP2) also prohibit solicitation for the purpose of monetary gain, that is, for making it one's occupation "to promote what society and the State consider to be an evil"?

Fornication, for example, must be tolerated, and so must gambling, but should a person be free to be a pimp, or to keep a gambling house? (98)

Mill says that these cases "lie on the exact boundary line" between toleration and repression. On the side of toleration, the mere fact of following an occupation and "living or profiting by the practice of it," does not of itself make it morally wrong or criminal.

> Society has no business as society, to decide anything to be wrong which concerns only the individual; that it cannot go beyond dissuasion, and that one person should be as free to persuade, as another to dissuade. (98)

On the side of repression, the public or the State, having decided that it is at least a disputable question that the activity (fornication or gambling) is bad, then "they cannot be acting wrongly" in endeavoring to exclude solicitors (pimps and owners of gambling houses) who admit to promoting the bad activity for their own financial interest only. Nothing would be lost, Mill says, by excluding the middle-man and letting people make their own private arrangements to satisfy their desire to fornicate or gamble.

> Thus (it may be said), although the statutes respecting unlawful games are utterly indefensible—though all persons should be free to gamble in their own or each other's houses, or in any place of meeting established by their own subscriptions and open only to the members and their visitors—yet public gambling houses should not be permitted. (99)

The 9th US Circuit Court of Appeals in San Francisco recently allowed a legal challenge to the statewide ban on prostitution to proceed. The ruling overturns a lower court's decision to toss the case out last year. During the Thursday hearing, conservative Judge Carlos Bea wondered aloud: "Why should it be illegal to sell something that it's legal to give away?" The plaintiffs argue that the 145-year ban "unfairly deprives consenting adults of the right to private activity, criminalizes the discussion of such activity, and unconstitutionally places prohibitions on individuals' right to freely associate." (Sugarman and White, 2017)

10.5 Self-enslavement

There is a liberty right "in any number of individuals" to join together in a common enterprise, "as long as the will of all the persons implicated remains unaltered," and as long as it is understood that when they do enter into such agreements, "it is fit, as a general rule, that those engagements be kept." (101).

The ground for not interfering with a person's voluntary act is "consideration for his liberty." There are exceptions to this rule, for example, no one can be held to an engagement that would involve harming a third party nor one that is injurious to themselves because it is assumed that what he or she chooses to do is desirable. Any other interference with his agreements are evidence that with he is pursuing what he believes to be good for him and so would violate the principle of individual liberty.

Selling oneself for a slave, or allowing oneself to be sold as a slave is a sales contract "that would be null and void, neither enforced by law or by opinion." (101)

> ...[B]y selling himself for a slave, he abdicates his liberty; he foregoes any future use of it beyond that single act. He therefore defeats, in his own case, the very purpose which is the justification of allowing to dispose of himself... The principle of freedom cannot require that he should be free not to be free. It is not freedom to be allowed to alienate his freedom. (101)

Mill's predecessor John Locke has the same conclusion but arrives at it from a different premise:

"He that cannot take away his own life, cannot give another power over it."

Being enslaved implies that the slave owners can do to you whatever they wish to do, including killing you. Hence, consent to being enslaved by another implies consent to your own destruction. But you do not have the liberty to destroy yourself. Only God has this power. Therefore, "you have not the liberty to enslave yourself to another." (Locke, §6, 17, 23).

10.6 Personal relationships and misplaced notions of liberty

Mill recognizes that there are important questions about individual liberty in marital and other familial relationships during the Victorian era in England.

10.6.1 Marriage in the mid-nineteenth century

In the same paragraph that he has the self-slavery discussion, Mill observes that the principle used there, governing freedom of contracts, "requires that those who become bound to one another in things which include no third party, should be able to release one another from the engagement" (102). Mill cites von Humboldt who recommends that this requirement should apply to personal relationships as well. Marriage, for example, "should require nothing more than the declared will of either party to dissolve it" (102).

Von Humboldt's recommendation that a married couple should have the right to dissolve their marriage without restriction was not adopted by any state or country until 1970. In that year, the state of California replaced the existing fault-based divorce requirement with a no-fault divorce procedure, in which it took only the consent of one of the parties to end the marriage. Most states in the U.S. now follow the California model. In England and Wales, however, anyone seeking a divorce must prove that their partner is at fault through adultery, desertion or unreasonable behavior. Alternatively, if both sides agree, they can part after two years of separation. (Houlgate, 2016, 191–193).

Mill is hesitant to agree with von Humboldt. He has two concerns. First, when one marries there is an express or tacit promise that one will act in a certain way and the married partners should be able to have reasonable expectations about their future. Moreover, there are frequently third parties that may soon become involved (new-born children) and this creates even more important obligations for the married couple.

But these concerns do not mitigate the most serious defects of marriage and family in mid-nineteenth century England. Mill argues that despite the obligation of the State to control the exercise of power that one person has over another, in the case of family relations this obligation is almost entirely disregarded.

> *The almost despotic power of husbands over wives needs not be enlarged upon here, because nothing more is needed for the complete removal of the evil than that wives should have the same rights and should receive the protection of law in the same manner as all other persons; and because, on this subject, the defenders of established injustice do not avail themselves of the plea of liberty but stand forth openly as the champions of power.*
> (103)

"In the eyes of the law (prior to 1882), once a woman married she basically ceased to exist. On her wedding day, she became one person with her husband and thereafter everything she did was under his direction. Once married she was under the complete and total supervision of her husband. Not only did he have control of all her possessions, he also had control over her body. Refusal of sex was grounds for annulment of the marriage. A husband was allowed to beat his wife, and even rape her, without fear of prosecution." (McBeath).

10.6.2 Parental obligations

In the case of children, "misapplied notions of liberty are a real obstacle to the fulfillment by the State of its duties" (103). A father regards his children, like his wife, as "a part of himself," and therefore, not to have his "absolute and exclusive control over them" interfered with.

This exercise of paternal power is most obvious in the case of education. Although it is "unanimously declared" that it is one of the "most sacred duties" to give to one's child "an education fitting him to perform his part well in life toward others and toward himself," there is no legal requirement for the father to make any "exertion or sacrifice for securing education to his child." It is left up to the father's choice to educate his child or not, even if it is provided free of charge! (104).

Mill argues that it is a "moral crime" to bring a child into the world if the parent (the father) does not fulfill his obligation to "not only provide food for its body, but instruction and training for its mind." The penalty for this serious omission is for the State to take over "at the charge, as far as possible, of the parent" (104).

Mill cautions that his recommendation applies only to the *enforcement* of education by the State, not that the State should take upon itself to direct that education. His reason for resisting a proposal that education should be entirely "in State hands," goes back to what he has earlier said about "individuality of character, and diversity in opinions and mods of conduct." Individuality requires diversity of education.

> *A general state education is a mere contrivance for holding people to be exactly like one another; and as the mold in which it casts them is that which pleases the predominant power in the government—whether this be a monarch, a priesthood, an aristocracy, or the majority of the existing generation—in proportion as it is efficient and successful, it establishes a despotism over the mind, leading by natural tendency over the body* (105).

> Over 90 percent of U.S. children in grades K-12 attend public schools. (Dynarski, 2014). In Great Britain, 93% of school age children attend public or "state schools" (Garner, 2015.) A private school in the U.S. is referred to in the U.K. as a "fee paying school," an "independent school" or sometimes a "public school."

State education, if it should exist at all, should be only one of many options available. The object of this is to set up a number of "competing experiences, carried on for the purpose of example and stimulus to keep the others up to a certain standard of excellence" (105).

Although education should be compulsory, the State should pay the costs of educating the children of those who are unable to pay. These children need not choose a State school but should have equal access to any number of schools offering "competing experiences" in education. The teachers who are qualified to provide education should be given sufficient remuneration for this task, and the government will pay these expenses, where necessary, on the assurance that the child's education is equally good in all schools and universities, private and public.

10.6.3 Justifiable restrictions on reproduction

Mill writes that *"one of the most responsible actions in the range of human being life is causing the existence of a human being."* This is because the consequence of reproduction "may be either a curse or a blessing," depending on whether the child "will have at least the ordinary chances of a desirable existence." To fail to do this "is a crime against that being" (106).

It is not only a crime against the child, but in an overpopulated country, unable to care for even the basic needs of its citizens, it is a "serious offense against all who live by the remuneration" they receive by their labor in a human labor-based economy.

Mill points out that it is not a violation of individual liberty for the State to demand that those who want to get married "show that they have the means of supporting a family" (107).

> Such laws are interferences of a mischievous act—an act injurious to others, which ought to be a subject of reprobation and social stigma, even when it is not deemed expedient to superadd legal punishment.

Mill is aware that any such proposal to prohibit procreation would be repelled as an attempt to put a restraint on the natural inclination to sexual intercourse, even if the parties to the marriage are made quite aware that the consequence of bringing a newborn into the world might be a "a life or lives of wretchedness and depravity" for the child.

> *When we compare the strange respect of mankind for liberty with their strange want of respect for it, we might imagine that a man had an indispensable right to do harm to others, and no right at all to please himself without giving pain to anyone.* (107)

There have been many attempts in history to prevent procreation. China introduced a "one child" policy in the late 1970s, to rein in the alarming rate at which the population was growing. In 1927, The U.S. Supreme Court, pronouncing that "three generations of idiots are enough," held that it is constitutionally permissible to force an intellectually challenged woman to have an abortion (*Buck v Bell*). There have been lawsuits filed in civil court by parents who claim that they wouldn't have conceived the child or would have aborted the fetus had they known "of the hereditary ailment or disability with which she was born" (FindLaw). And there have been proposals to require potential parents to obtain a license to have a child, using existing standards for licensing adoptive parents. The purpose of a child-bearing license is not to reduce population rates, but to reduce future incidents of child abuse by identifying potential child abusers before they procreate. (LaFollette, 1989).

10.7 Beneficent government: the welfare principle

Mill's final question is not about the limits of government interference with individual liberty but about the limits of promoting the welfare of individuals or groups. What are the justifiable limits of what government ought to do to promote the good of its citizens? The options are: either government doing something or causing something to be done for the people's benefit or "leaving it to be done by themselves, individually or in voluntary combination" (107).

The first option has been labelled "The Welfare Principle" (Feinberg, 33). Mill has three objections to the it, each grounded on utility.

First, if the thing to be done is likely to be better done by individuals rather than the government, then it ought to be done by individuals. Individuals are more likely to have a personal interest in the business, and this conduces to their being more fit than those whose interest is impersonal.

> This principle condemns the interferences, once so common, of the legislature, or the officers of government, with the ordinary processes of industry (107)

Second, even if the individuals may not do the particular thing as well as officers of government,

> ...it is desirable that it should be done by them, rather than by the government, as a means to their own mental education—a mode of strengthening their active faculties, exercising their judgment, and giving them a familiar knowledge of the subjects with which they are thus left to deal. (108)

Third, it is a "great evil" to add unnecessarily to the power of government.

> Every function superadded to those already exercised by the government causes its influence over hopes and fears to be more widely diffused, and convert, more and more, the active and ambitious part of the public into hangers-on of government. (109)

Notice that in each objection, Mill nowhere claims that government power is *inherently* evil. Each objection is based on predictable good consequences of limiting the power of government and the predictable bad consequences of extending its power over the individual.

Mill's final words are worth quoting:

> A government cannot have too much of the kind of activity which does not impede, but aids and stimulates, individual exertion and development. The mischief begins when, instead of calling forth the activity and powers of individuals and bodies, it substitutes its

own activity for theirs; when instead of informing, advising, and, upon occasion, denouncing, it makes them work in fetters or bids them stand aside and does their work instead of them. The worth of a State, in the long run, is the worth of the individuals composing it... (113).

But Mill makes no mention of two powerful passages from *Utilitarianism* that appear to contradict his dismissal of beneficent aid to struggling families.

First, after defining happiness (2.2.2.1), Mill observes that *"the present wretched education and wretched social arrangements are the only real hindrance to its [happiness] being attainable by all."* He says nothing about how these hindrances are to be removed by the unfortunate people alone without some help from government. He was certainly aware, for example, that there was no publicly funded elementary education in industrial or rural areas during in the mid-nineteenth century. At the time that Mill was writing *Utilitarianism* and *On Liberty*, there was nothing even close to an equal opportunity for these children. They were not provided the means to achieve the best life they are capable of achieving. If "individual exertion" gets poor families nowhere because of existing social impediments, then "informing, advising and denouncing" these families will be useless. What good is "mental sharpening" if you die of starvation or a curable disease in the process?

Second, Mill prides himself on what he sees as the affinity of the golden rule to the ethics of utility. He writes that "'To do as you would be done by,' and 'to love your neighbor as yourself,' institute the ideal perfection of utilitarian morality" (*Util.*, 16–17). But does the golden rule imply a rejection of the Welfare Principle? "Love yourself," for a poor person with a family to support does not imply a recommendation that she should "go it alone" against the tremendous power of wealth and class that existed in England during Mill's time. It certainly does not rule out government offers of free education for children and a government "safety net" for those times when the parents are unable to earn income adequate to pay for food, health care and shelter. If the ideal perfection of the utilitarian morality would enjoin "that laws and social arrangements should place the happiness...of every individual as nearly as possible in harmony with the interest of the whole" (17), then utilitarians generally should not be averse to endorsing the Welfare Principle as a first step toward achieving that ideal.

10.8 Questions for thought and discussion

1. Why does Mill say that trade is a social act? How is this relevant to the harm to-others principle (HO2)?

2. Opioids are drugs that act on the nervous system to relieve pain. Continued use and abuse can lead to physical dependence, withdrawal symptoms and death due to overdose. The United States is in the middle of a serious opioid epidemic: 64,000 deaths recorded in 2016. 20,000 deaths were due to overdoses of a synthetic powerful opioid called fentanyl (Natl. Inst. On Drug Abuse).   Can the doctrine of individual liberty be used to justify prohibitions of this drug? What kind of prohibition? Social or legal? If legal, should the sale and use of opioids be made a criminal act?

3. If being drunk or being a slacker harms only the drunk or the slacker, then how does Mill justify at least some social or legal interventions in these choices of life style?

4. "Liberty is often granted where it should be withheld and withheld where it should be granted."   How does this apply to marriage, parent-child relations and other familial relationships?

5.   Mill does not discuss abortion or artificial methods of contraception.   What conclusions would he reach on the justification of these activities, using the principle of individual liberty?

6. Regarding the last two paragraphs of 10.7, should Mill adopt the Welfare Principle as an amendment to HO2?

References

Baum, Bruce. 2007. J.S. Mill and liberal socialism. Ed. N. Urbanati and A. Zakarias. *J.S. Mill's Political Thought: A Bicentennial Reassessment.* Cambridge University Press.

Buck v Bell, U.S. 274 U.S. 200 (1927).

Feinberg, Joel. 1973. *Social Philosophy.* Englewood Cliffs, New Jersey: Prentice-Hall.

Findlaw. Indecent Exposure. https://criminal.findlaw.com/criminal-charges/indecent-exposure.html Accessed on 5/15/2018.

Findlaw. Wrongful birth and wrongful life lawsuit. https://injury.findlaw.com/medical-malpractice/wrongful-birth-and-wrongful-life-lawsuits.html

Garner, Richard. 2015. Number of pupils attending independent schools in Britain is on the rise figures show. *Independent.* https://www.independent.co.uk/news/education/education-news/number-of-pupils-attending-independent-schools-in-britain-on-the-rise-figures-show-10215959.html

Houlgate, Laurence. 2016. *Philosophy, Law and the Family: A New Introduction to the Philosophy of Law.* Switzerland: Springer International.

_____. 2018. *Understanding John Locke: The Smart Student's Guide to Locke's Second Treatise of Government.* Amazon: Kindle Direct Publishing.

Lacewing, Michael. Mill on harm and offence. *Routledge.* http://documents.routledge-

interactive.s3.amazonaws.com/9781138793934/A2/Mill/MillHarmOffence.pdf
Accessed on 5/15/2018.

LaFollette, Hugh. 1989. Licensing parents. *Public Affairs Quarterly* (1):75–87.

Locke, John. 1690. *Second Treatise of Government.* Several editions.

McBeath, V.L. 2018. Blog: *Victorian Era Women's Rights.*
https://valmcbeath.com/victorian-era-womens-rights/#.WwCctyBlDIU

National Institute on Drug Abuse. 2016. Overdose death rates.
https://www.drugabuse.gov/related-topics/trends-statistics/overdose-death-rates

SHouse California Law Group. 2018. California DUI penalties, punishment and
sentencing. https://www.shouselaw.com/drunk-driving-penalties.html

Sugarman, Emily and Jeremy B. White. Prostitution could be legalized in
California after case is allowed to go forward. *Independent.* 20 October 2017.
https://www.independent.co.uk/news/world/americas/california-prostitution-
legalisation-sex-work-case-allowed-go-forward-a8011306.html

Bibliography for *On Liberty* and the Limits of Liberty

Archard, D., 1990. Freedom not to be free: the case of the slavery contract in J.S. Mill's On Liberty. *The Philosophical Quarterly*, 40: 453–65.

Arneson, R. 1979. Mill's doubts about freedom under socialism." in Copp 1979: 231–49.

_____. 1980. "Mill versus paternalism. *Ethics*, 90: 470–89.

_____. 1982, Democracy and liberty in mill's theory of government," *Journal of the History of Philosophy*, 20: 43–64.

Berger, F. 1984. *Happiness, Justice and Freedom: The Moral and Political Philosophy of John Stuart Mill*. Berkeley: University of California Press.

Brown, D.G. 1972. "Mill on liberty and morality," *Philosophical Review*, 81: 133–58.

Crisp, R., 1997. *Mill on Utilitarianism*. London: Routledge.

Devlin, P. 1965. *The Enforcement of Morals*. Oxford: Oxford University Press.

Dworkin, G. 1972. "Paternalism," reprinted in Dworkin 1997: 61–82.

_____(ed.). 1997. *Mill's On Liberty: Critical Essays*. Totowa, NJ: Roman and Littlefield.

Dworkin, R. 1977. *Taking Rights Seriously*. Cambridge: Harvard University Press.

Feinberg, J. 1984–88. *The Moral Limits of the Criminal Law*, 4 vols., New York: Oxford

_____1973, *Social Philosophy*. Prentice-Hall.

Hart, H.L.A. 1963. *Law, Liberty, and Morality*. Stanford: Stanford University Press.

Jacobson, D. 2000. Mill on liberty, speech, and the free society. *Philosophy & Public Affairs*, 29: 276–309.

Lyons, D., 1979. Liberty and harm to others. reprinted in Dworkin 1997: 115–36.

Rawls, J., 1955, Two concepts of rules. *Philosophical Review*. 64: 3–32.

Riley, J. 1991. One very simple principle. *Utilitas*, 3: 1–35.

_____ 1998. *Mill On Liberty*. London: Routledge.

Rosen, F. 2013, *Mill*. Oxford: Clarendon Press.

Ryan, A. 1988. *The Philosophy of John Stuart Mill*, 2nd ed., London: Macmillan.

Sayre-McCord, G., 2001, Mill's 'proof' of the principle of utility: A more than half-hearted defense," *Social Philosophy & Policy*, 18: 330–60.

Scanlon, T.M., 1972, A theory of freedom of expression," *Philosophy & Public Affairs*, 1: 204–26.

Singer, P., 1972, Famine, affluence, and morality," *Philosophy & Public Affairs*, 1: 229–43.

Skorupski, J., 1989, *John Stuart Mill*, London: Routledge.

– – –, (ed.), 1998b, *The Cambridge Companion to Mill*, Cambridge: Cambridge University Press.

Smart, J.J.C. and B. Williams, 1973, *Utilitarianism: For and Against*, Cambridge: Cambridge University Press.

Sumner, W., 1996, *Welfare, Happiness, & Ethics*, New York: Oxford University Press.

Ten, C.L., 1980, *Mill on Liberty*, Oxford: Clarendon Press.

Urmson, J.O., 1953, "An Interpretation of the Philosophy of J.S. Mill," reprinted in Lyons 1997, 1–8.

Part III Postscript

Chapter 11 Theory and method

This book is the third in a series that began with books on Plato and Locke. As with those two books, I thought it would be of some help to readers to compare Mill to his famous predecessors on their solutions to common problems in ethics and political philosophy and also to explain Mill's philosophical method in *Utilitarianism* and in *On Liberty*.

11.1 Ethical theory

Theories about what makes an action right or wrong usually fall into one of two major categories: **deontological** (from the Greek word *deon*, meaning "duty" or "obligation), and **teleological** (from the Greek word *telos*, meaning "end").

According to deontological theories, what makes an act right or wrong is inherent in the act itself. It can be determined by a direct consideration of the act and its situation, or by deducing this from some formal principle. For example, if Frederick makes a promise to return Ludwig's car by the end of the week and Frederick fails to do this, then one needs only to look at features of *the act itself* to determine whether what he did is morally wrong: for example, that it is an act that *breaks a promise*. Moreover, this act (breaking a promise) is wrong even if the consequences are good or desirable (suppose that by not returning the car at the appointed time, Frederick was able to transport a seriously injured person to the hospital for life–saving surgery.)

According to teleological theories, what makes an act right or wrong are the consequences (ends) of the act. Acts of breaking a promise are not inherently wrong. They are wrong only if they bring about bad or undesirable consequences. If Frederick must make a choice between keeping his promise to return Ludwig's car on time and using the car to save a life, then not only is it morally right for Frederick to break his promise to Ludwig, but he has an obligation to do this if saving a life produces more good than bad consequences than keeping his promise.

11.1.1 Mill and Locke

The utilitarian theory is a species of the teleological approach to ethics. According to Mill's **hedonistic** theory of life, the only things that are desirable (good) are so because they are "either a part of happiness or means of happiness." It follows that the promotion of happiness *must* be "the test by which to judge all human conduct" (*Util.* 18). Our fundamental obligation is to do the act that will bring about the greatest balance of happiness over unhappiness for the greatest number of people.

Mill classifies the *evidence and source* from which the utilitarian principle derives its authority as *inductive*. "Right and wrong, as well as truth and falsehood, are questions of observation and experience." Thus, one can only know that telling the truth is right by observing the consequences of telling the truth. One can only know that breaking a promise is wrong by observing the consequences of this act. Mill makes no claim that we can know *a priori* (*prior* to observation and experience) that an action is right or wrong.

There is a law of nature, according to Locke, and it "obliges everyone not to harm one another in their life, health, liberty and possessions" (*Second Treatise*, §6). An act is morally right only if it conforms to the obligations set by the law of nature, and morally wrong if it violates said obligations. How do we know this to be true? The evidence and source from which the natural law principle derives its authority is *intuitive*. This means that it can be known to be true *a priori*, "requiring nothing to command assent except that the meaning of terms" in the law be understood.

Mill also clashes with Locke on the existence of natural rights. Following Bentham, Mill argues that all rights are conventional (human-made). A right (like the right to life, or the right to liberty) is a valid claim against society to protect us from those who would attempt to harm us (in our life or liberty). If asked why society ought to protect us from these threats, the only answer we can give is "utility." Locke would probably agree with Mill's definition of a right as a "valid claim on society," but he would argue that what makes the claim valid is that it can be derived from a corresponding natural right. For example, one has a valid claim on society to protect him from thievery only because there is a natural right not to be harmed in this way.

Mill would respond that there is no such thing as a natural right (all rights are conventional). If rights are valid claims on the protection powers of society, then a natural right is also a valid claim, thus prompting the question "Why ought society protect us in this way?" If Locke should answer "Because we have a natural right to this protection" he is now arguing in a circle by assuming what he wants to prove.

Locke's natural law theory is deontological, although there are some passages in *Second Treatise of Government* that confound this classification. For example, in an early paragraph, Locke defines political power as the right of making and execution laws for the purpose of protecting property, but "only for the public good" (§3). This comports quite nicely with Mill's idea of rights as moral requirements which stand highest in the scale of social utility" (*Util.*, 62).

11.1.2 Mill, Socrates and Plato

Socrates and Plato are difficult to categorize. This is partly because unlike Locke and Mill, they are not interested in foundational moral principles, moral rules, rights, or obligations. It has been suggested by some scholars that what Socrates and Plato are attempting to discover is what makes a *person* just or unjust rather than what makes an *action* morally right or wrong. The *ethics of persons* demands a standard of virtue or excellence which persons can *aspire* to meet and will more or less succeed at meeting. Some people do better than others at this. They are *more just* or *more virtuous* than others. But the *ethics of actions* demands moral *rules* that one either violates or does not violate. There is no "more or less" with rules. One either breaks or does not break a rule.

Socrates tries to find a *standard* for measuring the virtuous person in Plato's early (Socratic) dialogues. In *Euthyphro,* the characters Socrates and Euthyphro attempt and fail to discover a definition of piety. In *Apology,* Socrates tries to convince the jury that an unjust person does more harm to himself than he does to the person to whom he is unjust. In *Meno,* Socrates and his friend Meno try and fail to find a definition of virtue. In each of these dialogues, Socrates insists that he although he knows nothing, he is wiser than anyone else in Athens because he *knows* (is aware) that he *does not know* the answers to his own questions, thereby adding at least one benchmark for the virtue of wisdom. He also famously declares in *Apology* that the unexamined life is not worth living, thereby giving the world an objective, aspirational standard for leading a life that is worth living.

Plato is much more ambitious. In *Republic,* he develops a standard for determining the conditions under which a person is either completely just, completely unjust or somewhere in between. An individual is completely just when each part of the soul is doing the work for which it is naturally suited and "each element within [the soul] does its own job where ruling and being ruled are concerned" (*Republic* 443b). [Plato elsewhere calls this the "kingly" soul (580b-c) and the "healthiest" of all mental conditions (444e)]. If a non-rational part of an individual's soul (for example, the appetitive part) that is not naturally suited to rule sometimes "strays" and attempts to rule the soul, then on those occasions, the individual fails to meet the standard for being a *completely just* person.

None of this has anything to do with action. We are not told (for example) that someone is a just person only if she has a history of doing what is morally right. Instead, Plato tells us that justice is a matter of what is happening to us *psychologically, in the soul.* It is the soul that is just. If the parts of the soul are doing their job, with reason being supreme, then we can predict that this person will never do anything morally wrong, for example, "embezzle gold or silver he had accepted for deposit, thefts, or betrayals of friends in private life, or of cities in public life" (442d-e).

However, having a history of doing what is morally right does not guarantee that one is a just person, because it could be that the motivation for doing the morally right act was to maintain one's good reputation in the community. This is the criticism of the character Glaucon, early in *Republic,* when he challenges Socrates to prove that justice belongs in "the finest class" of things that are good: things desired for their own sake as well as for the sake of their consequences. Maintaining one's reputation is a *consequence* of being just. But people are easily fooled (ask any savvy politician). It is possible to maintain a public reputation for being a just person, while at the same time getting away with injustice. Therefore, what Socrates must prove with his theory of justice in the soul is that justice is *desired for its own sake*, not only for the sake of its consequences. Socrates eventually responds that the reason justice in the soul is desired for its own sake is that the person who has achieved this psychological condition is *the happiest of all* (580b-c). Happiness is not a condition that one pursues for some other end. It is its own end. It is desired for itself.

Mill does not respond directly to Plato's theory of the soul. But he is interested in the question of what motivates a person to obey the dictates of a moral principle. Why would someone be compelled to conform her conduct to Mill's utility principle (which obliges everyone to do the act that promotes the greatest happiness for the greatest number)? Is it because we are motivated by hope for favor or fear of displeasure "from our fellow creatures or from the Ruler of the Universe" (*Util.*, 27). This is what Mill refers to as *external* motives, and these motives are to be found attached to any moral principle, including the utilitarian.

The other motive for adopting a principle of duty is *internal*. It is as "a *feeling* in our own mind; a pain, more or less intense, attendant on violation of duty..." (27). We call this feeling *conscience*. "Its binding force...must be broken through in order to do what violates our standard of right, and which, if we do nevertheless violate that standard, will probably have to be encountered afterwards in the form of *remorse* (28). Mill writes that the feelings of conscience and remorse are also attached to the utilitarian principle (see the discussion in Part I, 3.2).

As noted in 3.1, Plato does not use the words "conscience" or "remorse" to describe the internal motivation for being a just person. One wants to be a just person because she has *justice in the soul*, and this is the healthiest and happiest mental condition one could ever want to be in. The internal sanction for being unjust is not remorse or guilt but having a soul that is "full of slavery and illiberality." This is the condition of the tyrannical soul in which the individual who suffers from this condition is maddened by appetites and passions, while becoming "the most wretched" of all (578b).

It is as if Mill and Plato are talking at cross purposes. Mill is explaining the internal motivation for doing the morally right *act*, while Plato is explaining the internal motivation for being a just *person*. Plato attempts to make a connection between being or becoming a just person who can be counted on to do what is morally right. The connection might be made if there was a logical relationship between having a healthy soul and a propensity toward feelings of conscience and guilt, but there is nothing in *Republic* to show this. The person with the just soul is happy and healthy and apparently has no desire to do anything wrong. Hence, there is no occasion for the just person to ever feel the tug of conscience or the after-effect of guilt. She will know how to maintain a just soul, but this is because it is in her own best interest to do so, not because she has a feeling of conscience that exercises a "powerful internal binding force" on her behavior (*Util.*, 33). If she does contemplate doing something morally wrong (for example, telling a lie or breaking a promise), then she will take this as a symptom of an unhealthy soul and will take steps to correct it. She knows she can be happy only if the parts of her soul are in healthy balance with one another, each doing the task it is naturally suited to do.

Another common issue for Mill and Plato is whether to designate virtue as something desired as an end or as a means to an end. In Chapter IV, Mill accommodates the popular idea that virtue is desired as an end by proclaiming that virtue is *a part* of happiness. Although there was no "original desire of it," except as a means to happiness, virtue eventually became so strongly associated with happiness that virtue was felt as a "good in itself" (37). Mill adds to this the observation that the utilitarian "enjoins and requires" that children and all others be taught to love virtue "up to the greatest strength possible" as a way of ensuring the general happiness.

Would this satisfy Plato? There are some scholars who contend that Plato's position is that virtue is the *only* unconditional good and that happiness (pleasure) is "a conditional good that the virtuous person rationally incorporates into his life" (Russell, p. 9). This appears to turn the tables on Mill. Plato's position implies that there was an original desire for virtue, independent of any association of virtue with pleasure. Mill has argued that this is a psychological (if not a logical) impossibility. The only thing that is unconditionally good is pleasure or happiness. Hence, the only motive for wanting to be virtuous is that it is either a means to happiness or a part of happiness. It is happiness that leads us to embrace the life of virtue by making the love of virtue a part of our conception of happiness. And yet, perhaps none of this matters. Plato and Mill would both agree that virtue and happiness, linked together are essential to the good life.

11.2 Political theory

In his introduction to *Political Philosophy*, Alan Gewirth wrote that the chief concern of political philosophy is with "the most general moral questions of society and government" (4). One of these questions is about the limits of political power: "By what criteria is it to be determined what should be the extent of political power and what rights or freedoms should be exempt from political or legal control?" (4) This is the single question asked and answered by Mill in *On Liberty* and thus the only topic we will use to compare Mill with Locke and Plato in this section.

11.2.1 Mill and Locke on liberty

The moral criteria used by Mill to answer the question about the extent of political power is ultimately utilitarian. Any answer to a general question of political philosophy must show how it promotes or tends to promote the general happiness. Mill claims that the harm-to-others principle passes the utilitarian test. If we limit the political power of society over the individual to those acts that cause or threaten to cause harm to others while at the same time prohibiting society from interfering with all other types of behavior, then the greatest happiness will be attained. It is only when individuals are left free to make their own decisions about the opinions they wish to express and the kind of life they want to lead, so long as they do no harm to others, that they can develop their faculties of critical thinking, judgment and choice. These are the faculties all individuals need for self-development and self-realization, two essential elements of happiness.

Locke has a short chapter in *Second Treatise* on the extent of legislative power (XI). In it he writes that the extent or limits of legislative power is determined by the end of government: to protect and preserve property. Property is defined by Locke to include "life, liberty and possessions." The word "liberty" might give us reason to think that he would discuss freedom of thought and expression, association and life-style choices. But we would be wrong. Locke is interested only in the *rule of law* and the restrictions this places on those who make law. Thus, Locke writes that the legislative power "is not, nor can possibly be absolutely arbitrary over the lives and fortunes of the people" (*ST*, §135). Since they lacked these rights in the state of nature, they cannot create them when they entered into society. Second, the legislators cannot by "extemporary arbitrary decrees," otherwise they will suffer the same uncertainty about their property as they had in the state of nature. Third, legislators "cannot take from any man any part of his property without his own consent." Fourth, the authority to make law cannot be transferred from one person or body of persons to a different person or body of persons. This can only be done by the people, for it is the people or the majority thereof, who have supreme power in the commonwealth.

11.2.2 *Mill and Plato on liberty*

In *Republic* there is nothing good Plato has to say about freedom of speech for the individual. Part of the reason he despised democracy was that this type of governance is "full of freedom and freedom of speech... [and everyone has] license in it to do whatever he wants," including the right to "arrange his life in whatever way pleases him" (557b). In the ideal state, where only trained philosophers are permitted to rule, we can presume that this public license would be revoked. The legislative assembly will be disbanded. The philosopher-kings will be free to speak their mind to one another, but no one else will join their conversations about how best to rule the city-state, unless invited. We can also presume that laws will be passed prohibiting any speech that would threaten the delicate balance between the three classes: moneymakers, auxiliaries (soldiers), and guardians (rulers).

If Plato was one of the philosopher-kings of the ideal state, would he have revoked a "license to speak publicly" for his mentor Socrates, who was prominent among those who spoke their mind whenever they wished to do so? As a consequence of exercising this freedom, Socrates was tried, convicted, and executed for the crimes of corrupting the youth of Athens (by teaching them by his own example of critical thinking) and refusing to believe in the approved gods of the city. Are we to presume that this never would have happened in the ideal state because it will *not* be "full of freedom and freedom of speech," or because special public-speaking licenses will be given only to people who the rulers can trust? I doubt that Socrates would have subscribed to either of these proposals. He would have defied the authorities and continued his life-long quest to prove that the goddess was wrong when she said, "Socrates is the wisest man in all of Athens."

> The ancient Greeks had two concepts of free speech. *Isegoria* is the older. It literally means "equal speech in public." This refers to a public place where people can talk, including both in the marketplace (*agora*), and the political assembly (*ekklesia*).
> The other form of free speech is *parrhesia*, meaning "speaking freely or frankly," implying "openness, honesty, and the courage to tell the truth, even when it meant causing offense" (Bejan). The most prominent practitioners of *parrhesia* were philosophers "like Socrates himself who would confront their fellow citizens in the *agora* and tell them whatever hard truths they least liked to hear" (Bejan).

11.3 Mill's philosophical method

Mill's method of finding answers to the central questions of ethics and political theory are quite transparent. He is careful to lead the reader through each step of analysis. We begin with arguments taken from *Utilitarianism*.

11.3.1 Examples from Utilitarianism

The best examples of Mill's method are seen in his proof of the principle of utility. It is actually a combination of three sub-proofs. The first is the proof that happiness is desirable as an end. The second is that happiness is the only thing desirable as an end. The third is the proof that the promotion of happiness is the test by which to judge of all human conduct. Since we have critically examined each of these proofs (4.1, 4.2, 4.3), they shall not be re-examined here.

The next best examples of Mill's method are from Chapter II of *Utilitarianism* in which he clarifies the utilitarian theory by defeating several criticisms of the theory.

The swine argument, for example, accuses the utilitarian theory of life as being "utterly mean and groveling" because it proposes pleasure as the ultimate end or good. Pleasure is an ultimate end for swine and other beasts (the critic says), but hardly suitable for humans who have "nobler objects" to pursue than pleasure.

Mill responds that if it is true that the utilitarian theory of life is suitable only for swine, then the critic is assuming that humans are capable of no pleasures other than those of which swine are capable. The assumption is false. Humans get pleasure out of listening to a Beethoven symphony, looking at a van Gogh painting, taking an afternoon stroll through the woods, or eating dinner with crystal and candlelight. I have yet to see a pig sit through a Beethoven symphony, nor have I witnessed a human voluntarily eating slop with pigs out of a trough.

The method that Mill is using is a simple syllogism. He uses the critic's hypothesis as a first premise (the utilitarian theory of life is suitable only for swine). The second premise states an implication of the first premise (humans are capable of no pleasures than those of which swine are capable). The third premise falsifies the second premise (humans are capable of different pleasures than those of which swine are capable). This gets us to the conclusion (therefore, the utilitarian theory of life is *not* a doctrine suitable only for swine). Mill takes the further step that the utilitarian theory of life is suitable for humans, precisely *because* "pleasure" includes far more than the pleasures enjoyed by swine.

The method used by Mill is an application of *modus tollens,* a rule of logic stating that if a conditional statement ("if *p* then *q*") is accepted, and the consequent does not hold (*not-q*), then the negation of the antecedent (*not-p*) can be inferred. The first and second premise constitute the conditional statement. The third premise is the negation of the consequent of the conditional, and the conclusion tells us that negation of antecedent can be inferred (that is, the utilitarian theory of life is *not* a doctrine suitable only for swine).

Another example of Mill's philosophical method is his response to the critic who argues that the utilitarian standard is "too high for humanity." It is too much to expect a person to always act "from the inducement of promoting the general interest of society" (17). Mill's response is to seize on the word "inducement." It means "motive." Mill points out that the utilitarian principle does not require that persons act from any particular motive. The theory only requires that an action have consequences that promote the general interest of society, despite what might motivate them to do this.

The method Mill is teaching is clarification. His critic has committed what is known as the "straw man fallacy." The straw man in this case is the argument for the conclusion that utilitarianism requires persons to always be motivated by a desire to promote the greatest good for the greatest number. But this is not Mill's position. Thus, the critic is "attacking a straw man" argument, an argument that Mill never made. Mill avoids the criticism by simply clarifying his position.

Mill's clarification was rejected by an early reader of *Utilitarianism* who said that he had a counter-example. Since counter-examples have long been a part of philosophical method, Mill felt it incumbent to reply. As discussed earlier (2.2.3.1), the critic asks Mill to imagine a "tyrant" who rescues an enemy who jumped into the sea to escape from him. The tyrant saved him from drowning but only because he wanted to inflict upon him more exquisite tortures. Mill's critic asks, "Would it tend to clearness to speak of that recue as a 'morally right action'"? The answer is "No," thereby proving that motive is essential to the evaluation of an act as morally right.

Mill's response is that the rescue is only the first step of an act that has horrific consequences. If we look at the entire act and take account of the consequences, then the tyrant's act is morally wrong. And there is no need to consider the tyrant's motive in order to make this assessment.

The lesson to be learned here is that counter-examples are only as good as the original example it provides as a counter. The method of counter-example proves an argument invalid by generating an example of the given argument form with true premises and a false conclusion. Mill's thesis is that consequences, not motive determine the morality of an action. The counter-example is a case in which we are to conclude the opposite: that it is motive, not consequences that determine the morality of the action. But the critic's example of the tyrant does not show this. Instead, once we know that the tyrant has not only pulled his enemy from the sea but has also tortured him after getting him on board the ship, then this consequence alone proves that the conduct of the tyrant is morally wrong. His motive is irrelevant.

11.3.2 Examples from On Liberty

In her excellent introduction to the 1978 Hackett edition of *On Liberty*, Elizabeth Rappaport wrote that the procedure used by Mill to respond to criticisms of the first version of the harm-to-others principle is "a model of open philosophical inquiry." She goes further and says that the entire essay "can be regarded a textbook on how to conduct philosophical inquiry as Mill conceived it, a test that teaches by example, as much as it is a treatise on liberty" (xvi).

Let's look at the examples again and see what there is to learn about philosophical method.

The first version of the harm-to-others principle says that "the only conduct of anyone ... which merely concerns himself, his independence is, or right, absolute. Over himself, over his own body and mind, the individual is sovereign" (9). But Mill immediately sees a problem with this: "whatever affects himself may *affect others* through himself" (11). Except for hermits and people who live alone on small distant islands, almost everything we do when we emerge from our house or apartment and mingle in society will affect or concern others in some way. There is no bright line that separates other-regarding and self-regarding conduct.

The method Mill uses to criticize his own theory is (once again) the method of counter-example. If one person physically assaults another, this is a clear case of other-regarding conduct. If the same person wears a T-shirt with the words "F*ck You" emblazoned on it, this also may be classified as other-regarding if others find this message to be offensive, thereby blurring the line between self-regarding and other-regarding conduct.

Mill must find a way to provide a plausible repair to the harm-to-others principle. The aim is to create a bright line that will allow those who use the principle to make clear determinations about harms society ought to protect its members against and harms that society ought to tolerate (Rapaport, xvii).

Mill's solution is to revise the harm-to-others principle by narrowing the scope of the word "harm," in accord with the dictates of the utilitarian principle. He does this by declaring that the only harms (concerns, interests) that society ought to protect us against are those that violate our rights (see section 9.1.2 *supra*) Thus, in the T-shirt case, if someone today sees the shirt and says that she finds the words on the shirt to be "offensive," she cannot claim that her rights have been violated. There is no right (in twenty-first century America) not to have one's sensibilities about decency offended by the public display of certain words, nor ought there to be a legitimate claim or obligation which the T-shirt wearer is bound to honor [but see 10.3 for Mill's discussion of standards of decency in the mid-nineteenth century].

Assuming that we now know how to distinguish harm to others from harm to self, another objection to it is from those who argue that "society has an obligation in some instances to prevent people from harming themselves." The examples they offered are requirements to wear seatbelts when driving an automobile, to wear certified helmets when riding a motorcycle, to obtain certification to use and purchase certain poisons, or to use certain explosives (like dynamite), to obtain a doctor's prescription to purchase certain pharmaceuticals, and not to use heroin and other listed addictive drugs on pain of fines or incarceration.

In most of these examples there is no "distinct and assignable person" who can plausibly declare that their rights have been violated by someone's failure to do what is required (9.1). You have not violated *my* right not to be harmed if *you* fail to wear your seatbelt. You might have put yourself in danger, but I cannot show that you have an obligation *to me* unless I am a dependent family member, or you have some other distinct and assignable obligation to others that would require you to wear a seatbelt.

There is one proviso that Mill makes about the use of dynamite, poisons and (we can assume) would also make for potentially harmful drugs (e.g. opioids). It is legitimate to require certification or require a prescription because no one would voluntarily injure or harm themselves by using or ingesting these things. We can guarantee that the use will be *voluntary* by labelling the explosive and the poison, requiring an official certificate for their use, and (in the case of pharmaceuticals) have a physician explain the safe use of the drug.

But if we are assured that individuals are aware of the risks they are taking, and are not violating the rights of others, then Mill would argue that society has no business in prohibiting their self-regarding conduct. If asked why society ought not to interfere, Mill would give his standard reply (previously quoted at 7.5). First, there is no certain truth to which all should adhere, especially in ethics or political theory.

Mankind are not infallible; that their truths for the most part, are only half-truths; that unity of opinion, unless resulting from the fullest and freest comparison of opposite opinions, is not desirable and diversity not an evil, but a good...

Second, happiness can only be achieved through self-development and self-realization.

As it is useful that while mankind are imperfect, there should be different opinions... [T]here should be different experiments of living; that free scope should be given to varieties of character, short of injury to others; and that the worth of different modes of life should be proved physically, when anyone thinks fit to try them. It is desirable, in short, that in things which do not primarily concern others individuality should assert itself. (54).

11.3.3 Summary

The stated purpose of the *Smart Student's Guide* series is to not only understand the works of some of the great Western philosophers but to understand philosophical method. One lesson is that there is and should be no mystery about these methods. They are no more than the application of logic to the central problems of ethics and political philosopher. John Stuart Mill, like Plato and Locke, is not a mystic or seer who seeks revelation to solve philosophical problems. He applies standard argument forms like *modus ponens* or *modus tollens* to determine validity. He appeals to *counter examples* and searches for fallacies like the *straw man* or *reductio ad absurdum* to test not only the arguments of others but his own arguments as well.

Mill fully realizes that he does not always get it right. He even admits as much in *On Liberty* when he recognizes the necessity to revise his signature principle, thereby showing us that he embodies the spirit of the true philosopher: **Always be a *seeker* of truth, never assuming you have found it.**

References

Bejan, T.M. 2017. The two clashing meanings of free speech. *The Atlantic.*
https://www.theatlantic.com/politics/archive/2017/12/two-concepts-of-freedom-of-speech/546791/

Gewirth, Alan. 1965. *Political Philosophy.* New York: Macmillan.

Parry, Richard. 2014. Ancient Ethical Theory. *The Stanford Encyclopedia of Philosophy.* Edward N. Zalta (ed.).
https://plato.stanford.edu/archives/fall2014/entries/ethics-ancient/

Rapaport, E. 1978. Introduction. Rapaport. E. (ed.) John Stuart Mill. *On Liberty.* Hackett.

Russell, Daniel C. 2005. *Plato on Pleasure and the Good Life*. Oxford: Oxford University Press.

Glossary

A posteriori	Knowledge based on (posterior to) observation and experience.
A priori	Knowledge not based on (prior to) observation and experience.
Considerations	Reasons for giving one's assent to a theory or doctrine, in lieu of a direct proof.
Direct proof	A logical deduction from premises to conclusion (see Deductive argument).
Consequentialism	Ethical theories contending that an action is right or wrong only because of the consequences or ends of the action. (see also *Teleological*).
Deductive argument	An argument or proof in which the author claims certainty for the conclusion
Deontology	Ethical theories contending that an action is morally right because of some characteristic of the action itself, not because the consequences or ends of the action are good.
Epicureanism	After a school founded in Athens by Epicurus. The school advocated hedonism but contended that mental pleasure was qualitatively better than physical pleasure. "The ultimate pleasure was held to be freedom from anxiety and mental pain, especially that arising from needless fear of death and of the gods." (Cambridge)
Hedonism	The theory that pleasure is the highest good and proper aim of human life (see also Epicureanism).
Inductive argument	An argument in which the author claims probability (not certainty) for the conclusion.
Inductive school	A theory of ethics claiming that right and wrong can only be known through observation and experience (see *a posteriori*).
Intuitive school	A theory of ethics claiming that right and wrong can be known through intuition, independently of observation or experience (see *a priori*).
Optimific	Producing the maximum good consequences.
Prima facie	An obligation or duty that we have *on the face of it*, meaning that it may be overridden by another duty that applies to the same act. A *prima facie* duty is not absolute.

Sanction	A motive or "binding force" for obedience to a moral principle (Mill).
Teleological	Ethical theories contending that an action is right or wrong only because of the consequences or ends of the action. (see Consequentialism).

28510043R00085

Made in the USA
Lexington, KY
16 January 2019